Robert R. Manners

Cuba

And other verse

Robert R. Manners

Cuba
And other verse

ISBN/EAN: 9783337378059

Printed in Europe, USA, Canada, Australia, Japan

Cover: Foto ©Thomas Meinert / pixelio.de

More available books at **www.hansebooks.com**

CUBA,

AND OTHER VERSE,

BY

ROBERT MANNERS.

Here pause my gothic lyre a little time;
The leisure hour is all that thou canst claim.
—*Beattie.*

TORONTO:

WILLIAM BRIGGS,
29–33 RICHMOND STREET WEST,
1898.

ERRATUM.

On page 17, line 8, for "looks" read "shocks."

CONTENTS.

ERRATUM.

On page 17, line 8, for "looks" read "shocks."

IV.   CONTENTS.

What is writ is writ: would it were worthier.
                                          —Byron.

CUBA.

CUBA.

I.

The *Indies'* seas—resplendent, sapphire-bright;
The coral lands where Nature ever smiles,
Where summer reigns, throned on a thousand isles,
Crowned as befits the queen of life and light.
The tropic sun—a fire which knows no wane,
Uplifting life in opulence sublime,
In endless wealth; the eminent domain
Of life spontaneous from creation's prime!
Clad in rich tints or robed in fiery hues
Its myriad forms in plant, in fruit, and flower;
Munificence supreme; supremest power
Revealed in never-wearying love profuse.
The sum unspeakable, and soul and sense
Gaze wonder-bound before Omnipotence!

As neighboring trees all blossom-laden rest
'Mid the rose-haze of summer's sultry day,
So lie those isles upon the sun-flushed breast
Of southern seas where spicy breezes play.

7

Balmful those winds with fragrant sweets imbued,
Culled from unnumbered fruits and floral blooms,
Profusely rich, which scatter their perfumes
Upon the air—o'erfilled to lassitude.

Unceasingly amid the island shades
Pours the glad music of the plumaged throng,
Most joyous heard 'mid the secluded glades
Of the wild-wood, where they betimes prolong
Into the silence of the night their song.

Entrancing scenes of artless luxury!
Where bounteous nature has profusely shed
Her rarest gifts, nor deem on earth can be
Scenes where her beauties are more richly spread.

Yet, 'mid those scenes, in sullen grandeur rise
Mountainous steeps, wild-cragged, their forms sear-
    browned,
Which boldly reach majestic toward the skies,
Their towering crests with dark-plumed pines en-
    crowned!
Upon their heights the island mountaineer,—
In view the waters of th' encircling sea,—
Makes his abode; his joy their crags to dare;
Nor deems he else an equal luxury,
Though 'neath his feet unfading shades abound,
And fruits delicious freight the hidden ground.

Such beauty theirs—those isles of *Indies'* sea;
Such riches theirs as tempt cupidity!

II.

The morn across Antilles seas
Broke softly with a cradling breeze,
Which o'er the slumbering waters crept
Till lost in island groves it slept,
Or wandered merrily along
Amid its shades, which, at its song
Waking, their 'leafy banners' hung
Out as it passed, while sweetly sung
The plumaged choir in bright array,
Their anthem to returning day.
To these and opening woodland flowers,
To lakelets bright, in verdant bowers
Embosomed, the glad zephyrs spoke
Their greetings, and all nature woke
To joy; the sylvan wavelets kissing
From sleep; with smiles them dimpling o'er,
Or from their cradled rest enticing,
To leave them sighing on the shore!

III.

The sun, now risen, through the verdured trees,
Tuned by the breeze to rustic symphonies,
Shed o'er a woodland lake,—whose waters lie

Among the hills that overlook the sea,
Carribean named, where round the southern coast
Of Cuba's isle it circles, eastward lost,—
Its softest rays, yet brightest till its breast
Sparkled with brilliants, like some beauty dressed
In jeweled splendor, as it rose and fell
In warm pulsation, softly audible.
Upon its wooded slopes, here long alone,
Save for his child,—scarce to his household known,
In solitude had dwelt and slept—now dead—
The Count Zambrana.   Many years had fled
Since first he sought the shades which now waved o'er
His marble crypt upon the farther shore.
Whence he had come none knew, none e'er had known;
Why thus he lived, avoiding e'en his own,
And none remembered since the earliest day
He sought those hills one from them spent away,
Though at each eve this man of mystery
Had loved to wander by the neighboring sea;
And only there was he e'er known to show
Aught of emotion; then from some deep woe
It seemed to rise, which in his heart lay sealed,
Some wearing secret, jealously concealed.
Stern was his glance, withal yet kind his eye
Where pride enthroned maintained a mastery
O'er those emotions which his heart down-weighed,
Nor rose unguarded, save when sleep betrayed.
In life, his thought ne'er wearying did employ

Itself in studying but his daughter's joy;
And wealth possessed, left her naught to desire,
Save to reclaim from that dark shade her sire,—
Was it remorse or sorrow which thus moved
The heart her own so truly, fondly loved.
But Death—that presence which man's heart subdues,
Refusing oft that which alone it sues
In life's last hour: a moment's strength to bear
Up from its tomb the sins Pride buries there—
Had sought Zambrana, and its swift decree
Forever sealed his life's strange mystery.
Now years had fled; to womanhood had grown
The child, yet had she not been left alone,
For a not less than mother's love was hers
In one her guardian from her earliest years.

IV.

Upon the woodland lake, smooth gliding o'er
Its waves, a gondola approached the shore,
Beneath the oar of swarthy Islander
Borne gently onward. Long his raven hair
Fell from beneath a ribboned sombrero
About his neck uncovered, and below,
Across his half-bared breast of olive hue,
Floated before the breeze. His eyes—but who
Would paint a Criollo and shade his eyes
Less dark than are his southern starlit skies!
A lovely figure in the boat reclined:

Zambrana's daughter; her fair form, confined
In whitest folds of softest texture, lay
The paragon of grace and symmetry,
Beneath a silk o'ershading, on a spread
Of Persian tapestry. Rested her head
On her warm hand, round which her wealth of hair,
In dark profusion fell; and naïvely there
A crimson blossom clung, and seemed to seek
To shade the damask softness of her cheek.
Her eyes were dark—'twould be a mockery
To try to paint them by a simile,
As they beneath their silken fringe, half closed,
In lustrous languor, dreamingly reposed.

A terraced stair, with marble balustrade,
Rose from the lake, and thence an avenue,
'Neath palms o'er-arching, stretched up the hill-side
To where, crowning its summit, the chateau
In simple beauty stood. Around the shade
Of tamarind, ceiba and the mango swayed
In wandering winds, laden with sweets distilled
From neighboring fruity groves, while clustering there
Bloomed floral hues unnumbered, and the air,
Amid the foliage musical, was filled
    With songs of birds.

Entrancing scenes stretched round on every hand,
Far as the sight the vista could command

In azure framed—the vast circumference
With beauty stored; a glow of life intense:
Here orange groves displayed their wondrous yield
In golden clusters o'er the verdured field;
There softly white the coffee beauty spread
Her flake-like blossoms fringed with gentlest shade
Of stately palms, which 'mid the slumbrous air
Reposeful stood—majestic everywhere.
Beyond, empurpled, 'gainst the luminous sky
A mountain range in sombre majesty
Stretching far eastward with the boundless sea,—
August joint-tenants of immensity.

Near the chateau, 'neath an embowering shade,—
A net of verdure with bright blossoms spread,—
Where over-arching vines, with blooms o'er-run,
Tempered the brightness of a tropic sun,
Reclined the figure of a youth, though grown
To manhood's stature.   Through the screen o'er-
      thrown,
Of foliage intertwined, the sunlight crept,
Lighting his brow, as motionless he slept,
O'er which his hair, in indolent unrest,
Moved in dark clusters, by the breeze caressed.
A flush was warmly glowing on his cheek
As soft as are the mellow tints that streak
The summer sky, when, as night's curtains close,
On twilight's breast, day sinks into repose.

Yet there was stamped upon his placid face
Courage and pride, all tempered with a grace
Of true nobility, that influence
Which moulds the face in gentler lineaments.
Plain were his features, yet enthronéd there,
With stateliness, appeared that nameless air
Of conscious force,—the reflex of a mind
Which still attracts and which commands mankind;
The superscription of that power that sways
The world, the *mind*,—sovereign of sovereignties!
With its great premier, governing reason, throned,
Controlling worlds, yet by no power bound.
Its consort thought; the eye its minister;
The universe its realm; the arbiter
In man of men, who, envious, then behold
Themselves resistless by its power controlled,
As in submission, 'neath its master spell,
They render homage, though their wills rebel!

V.

From midnight till the star of morn
Paled 'neath the saffron veil of dawn,
Young Pasco, o'er the star-lit wave,
By many a cape and island cave,
Full many a league along the shore
Guided his boat with steady oar,
From where, within a cliff-bound bay,

A band of Cuban patriots lay
Close 'neath a friendly mountain wall
Which stretched around, impassable.

There in the fastness of the mountain height,
Dreading naught else save the betraying night,
His patriot comrades waited for the day
When once again their hands should rend away
Another thong that bound their bleeding land,
Wrenched from her heart-strings by a tyrant's hand.

*   *   *   *

Thou stricken isle! how long shall Slaughter flood
Thy vales of beauty with the patriots' blood;
How long still, struggling, must thou bleed, nor find
One hand of mercy thy red wounds to bind?
Weakest yet braver than the strongest all,
Must freedom's fairest child unheeded call,
And to the accents of her anguished cry,
Hear no response, though many strong be nigh.
Thou guardian Genius of the patriot brave!
Hear thou thy sons—still thine the power to save—
Who to thee turn, scourged in their native land
For freedom's cause by an aggressor's hand.
Hear thou thy sons who nobly there defy
Thy bitterest foe, freedom's arch-enemy;
That chief of despots, whose long history reads
A record dark of persecution's deeds,

Who now oppressing that unhappy clime
Would there proscribe e'en liberty a crime—
That gift divine, hereditary right,
From mankind stolen in oppression's night!
Withhold no longer thine avenging sword;
Nay, they are free, if thou but speak'st the word,
That word unsaid, lo, each returning day
Beholds them crushed anew by tyranny!
Stay in their course the crimson reeking blade
And kindling brand, by fell destruction swayed,
Which o'er that land, where all's so wondrous fair
Spread blackened desolation and despair.
See, 'mid the verdure of his native glade,
Attacked by panther, from its ambush strayed,
The noble stag, just struggling to his feet,
Defiantly fronts his pursuer's hate.
Now on his foe impetuously he flies,
A desperate courage flashing from his eyes;
The beast recoils, then with a fierce rebound
Springs at its victim; half borne to the ground
His antlers stout receive his savage foe:
With cry half pain, half hate, back crouching low.
Yet once again behold him full at bay,
Dauntless—
      Till now his panting breaths betray
His sinking frame, which scarce may long sustain,
The brave, proud spirit which it bears within.

See on the jaws of his fierce assailant
The scarlet life, in savage cunning rent·
From his torn limbs, that know no soothing balm
Save the soft currents of his life-blood warm;
Yet not alone *his* flows; mark the red dye
His antlers bear, drawn from his enemy!
Lo, Cuba thus confronts Hispania still,
With courage not her fiercest looks can kill,
Though stricken bleeding—
                              Thou America!
Strong as thou art and pledged to liberty,
Thus at thy gates shall stranger masters slave
Thy sister—loveliest child that Nature gave!
Thy freedom viewed, she in thy steps would tread,
Yet stones thou giv'st her where she asks but bread.
Nay, while her cries now smite thy sluggard ear,
Cries thou know'st well, for once thine own they
        were,
While in her flesh, all quivering, deeper gnaw
Beneath thine eyes, the chains her enslavers draw,
Wilt thou, O mother!—canst thou close thy heart?
Must thus the prestige of thy name depart ?
A Nemesis arise, clothed in thy might,
With justice armed, thy countenance alight
With righteous vengeance, so shall tyranny
Before thy face in terror shrink away,
As to its lair the preying beast of night,
When o'er the mountain beams the morning light!

The people's voice is God's, the old world said;
The nation's voice shall rule, the new hath shown,
And now it speaks and bids thee grant thine aid
To save those struggling for a cause thine own!
No longer wait—each day thou dost abstain
The plagues of famine, fire and death increase,
And worse than death for those who shall remain
Unless thou bidst the tyrant's sway to cease.
Hear, then, Columbia—this thy mandate be:
The western lands from despots shall be free.
Lead thou the way, thy meteor flag unfurled;
Be freedom's foremost champion of the world.

        *   *   *   *

Young Pasco, boldest of the brave,
Feared not the wildness of the wave;
To him the night wind o'er the sea
Was but a voice of melody;
Its tossing waves—his heart more free—
Were but a thing of ecstasy
In which his boundless thoughts but found
Companions; their impatient sound
Reflecting in their wild unrest,
Love's fevered pulses in his breast;
And so he welcomed with delight
These restless spirits of the night.
Naught did he fear, for to the heart
That knows the strength love's throbs impart—
A strength in dangers stronger proving
That stand betwixt the loved and loving—

There is no peril which can fright
On surging wave or mountain height,
While depths of fondest happiness
Await the heart in love's embrace!
Now, as the dying shades of night
Fled silently before the light
Of coming day, his light caïque
Was moored within an island creek.
Soon reached the scene he knew so well,
Made sacred by the last farewell
Which he had kissed from lips that thrilled
His quickening pulse, though parting chilled
His anxious heart—for love e'er dreads
The cloud a lowering future spreads,
Though o'er the star of hope may gleam
With bright albeit uncertain beam;
A brightness which its spirit fears
Reflected in a woman's tears.
Fatigued, now 'neath a shade reclined
He sought a while of rest to find,
Before the fast returning day
Should bring the hour that should repay
Love's willing toil.   Soon kindly sleep
His eyelids closed, as the calmed deep,
Just 'neath the hill whereon he lay,
Low whispering of tranquility,
Soothed weariness to sweetest rest,
While fancy, for love, fondly traced
In dream-tints, scenes where only joy
Admitted, bore love company!

VI.

As in the loadstone dwells a vital force
We may not trace to its mysterious source,
Which seeks its consort, the responding steel,
And to it clings, nor why does it reveal,
Th' effect we mark;—the *cause?* There dies the light,
And Wonder pauses on the verge of night,
While all the cunning of philosophies
Ends in the simple knowledge that *it is!*

E'en thus in love a nameless power lies,
Attracting still its own affinities,
Beneath which force the heart responsive moves
Love's willing footsteps toward the soul it loves:
The will obeys,—and why it cannot tell,
Itself surrendering to that mystic spell,
In spirit prescience which outwings the sight,
The soul subjective in its unseen flight.

Thus dawns upon the light of consciousness
    Love's guiding star,—pure and serene its glow,
When near us throbs the heart our own would bless,
    Feeling ere yet its presence we may know;
'Tis but divined—this intercourse of souls;
    Unknown, its workings to the mists of sense,
And yet the will its magic force controls,
    Which moves responsive to its influence.

Now, as she wandered 'neath the verdant shades
    Which round her island home luxuriant pressed,
As from the lake she sought their quiet glades,
    Dreaming of one whose image filled her breast,
Did Lolo feel this influence which invades
    The realm of thought, with pulses to invest
Those chords magnetic which two hearts unite:—
A bond too hallowed for the sensual sight.

And thus impelled, unconsciously she sought
    The floral shade where Pasco sleeping lay,
Wondering the while if life could offer aught
    And Pasco gone; and then in ecstasy
Transfixed she stood, as quick that saddening
        thought,
    Darkening her eyes, faded in tears of joy:—
And oh how bright beamed her all-lustrous eyes
'Neath that one cloud, flashing love's sympathies.

" My Pasco! "—and her voice sank sweetly lower
    From the first pulse of love's temerity,
Like the lone nightingale's, in twilight's hour,
    As, when disturbed, its warblings die away;
And flushed her cheek as, like an arching flower,
    O'er him she leaned in love's expectancy,
Pressing her heart which throbbed all envious,
That sleep should claim a moment of its bliss.

O Love, thou strange enigma of the soul!
   Fearless yet fearful; all-seeing yet how blind;
Omniscient yet thou spurn'st the just control
   Of thy co-dweller Reason.   Thus combined,
Opposing forces blend a marvellous whole
   In thy mysterious framework, that designed
By goodness infinite that from its height
The soul might glimpse th' elysian fields of light.

E'en as to thought, to sight dost thou impart
   By thy mysterious force higher virtue
Supernal, giving all things to the heart,
   By vision there revealed, an aspect new;
Clothed in new beauty all; beauty no art
   Hath cunning to resolve, while that we knew
Before as happiness, to thee doth seem
But like the baseless fancies of a dream!

Employs which once no joy could e'er impart,
   Or longings waked they could not satisfy,
'Neath thy sweet force awake within the heart
   Throbbings of all-sufficing ecstasy.
Heaven's richest dower to man; of life the part
   Most sacred; flame of immortality,
Which here below sheds its celestial light,
Without which life were lifeless, day were night.

No longer able to resist, Lolo,
   Beside him seated 'mid the flowers, now

A gently lingering kiss upon his brow
  In maiden fervor pressed; then back she drew,
As fearing love too bold, while a warm glow
  Suffused her cheek; then o'er his face anew
Her own she leaned, as Pasco, waking, seemed
As if he doubted if he lived or dreamed.

"Is it a dream? No, no! No dream could trace
Such wondrous beauties as my Lolo grace;
No vision paint an image half so fair
As thou, my idol,—and thou sought me here?
Thou Beauty's self!" Then, in one long embrace
Upon his breast pillowed her lovely face,
In speechless joy her idoled form he pressed
Close to the heart that trembled in his breast.

"Not here, my Pasco—everywhere this heart
In spirit-flight hath followed where thou wert,
At morn and eve, and through night's visions still
The paths exploring of each neighboring hill,
As hope still promised with each coming day
Thy watched return—how oft but to betray;
And when its voice with less assurance came,
While busy memory ceaseless called thy name,
Love, trembling, sank on sorrow's pallid breast,
And there, disconsolate, sobbed itself to rest.
But this no more; sorrow shall wait on joy,
Which must alone the hours now employ

With thy return, thou truant wanderer;
And first account thee since we parted here.
Then didst thou promise, by thine own true heart,
E'en thus: 'but for a little time we part;'
And now the moon, then newborn, hung on high,
Full thrice hath waned along the summer sky.
And see!—why thus in military mien
Art thou returned?   Where hath my Pasco been,
That thus of dress, as for some carnival,
Absence has been so strangely prodigal?
'T is sure thy humor,—yet thy pensive eye
Scarce seems to bear such presence company."

"Then with thine own softly persuasive eyes,
Shall they but bear love's happier embassies:
E'en as thou say'st: 'sorrow on joy shall wait,'
As love would sorrow e'er anticipate
Which still o'erbodes; while 't is but joy to weigh
In love's sweet balance sorrows passed away.
Called from thy side, still in our country's cause,
The cause of justice and of freedom's laws
Employed each hour,—too brief to liberty,
Yet oh, how lengthened distant far from thee,
Would 't were not mine to tell thee that in vain
Our land still struggles 'neath oppression's chain;
That still her sons must strive, nor free her soil
From despots who her of her rights despoil.
Come now the hour when all who love their isle,

As hating those who still her vales defile,
Must strike for freedom, nor e'en shrink to bear
Its standard foremost in the ranks of war."

"Thou hast already nobly borne thy part,
Allegiance sharing but with this fond heart,
My Pasco, till of all thou once possessed—
All save thy life, in this art thou divest."
"That gift alone is worthy freedom's cause,—
Her voice reproachful till each patriot draws,—
And if but ventured, on that hazard cast,
Rich the reward, if that loved cause at last
Triumphant stands; and if this may not be,
Better to die than live for tyranny.
But of thyself : first would I hear thee tell
Of the time past which thou hast marked so well
By the chaste moon, which now thy constancy
Shall ever witness, near or far from thee."
Then were recalled those hours of bitterness
When hope beamed low, those tremblings of distress
Which rend the heart when separation flings
Dark, chilling shadows from its sombre wings.
Each day remembered with its train of fears;
Patience grown weary, faith subdued to tears,
Fond expectation at the morning light
Waking in smiles; in tears ere came the night,
While morn and night hope watched unwearyingly,
To soothe the pain of love's despondency.

Now in the brightness of joy's warmthful ray
Dissolved in light, each shadow passed away,
As 'neath the sun the mists of morning fade
Which ere the dawn, earth's slumbering beauty
        shade.

*   *   *   *

The hours had sped,—how swiftly do they fly,
Unmarked by thought in love's sweet company,—
Till now they led past the meridian height
In robes of gold-edged fleece the god of light.
Though marked the hour, yet still did Pasco fear
To hope and love-expectant to declare
Honor's last act, for well he knew that this
Quick must consign sweet joy to bitterness.
But now, 'neath Time's injunction, in his heart
The pain that soon—fore'er perhaps, they must part,
For utterance pressed, as thus again to thought
Memory recalled his grief, in joy forgot.
Then as some cloud which 'neath the moon's pure
        light
Suffused with brightness, decks the brow of night,
When swept away by spirit winds, that sigh
Their weird lamentings through the silent sky,
To darkness fades, thus borne from its bright sphere
Into the regions of the nether air,
Shadowing o'er the watching stars, but now
Beaming in beauty on its silvery brow,

So the glad light which shone in Pasco's face,
Reflected from love's fervent happiness,
Faded away as now within his breast
Grief's gathering mists their chilling darkness pressed,
And spread a shade of anguish o'er his brow
Which beamed so bright with happiness but now.

But quick his heart again forbade that this
Should shadow o'er his star of loveliness,
As it dispelled the cloud which thought had thrown
Across his face,—yet ere 't was wholly gone,
Her upturned eyes, then fixed upon his own,
With love's perception marked that shadow fade,
Which to her own his troubled heart betrayed.
Then thus she spoke: " My Pasco, must I trace
One line of sadness falling o'er thy face,
Nor know the sorrows which thy heart invade,
And thus the brightness of thine eyes o'ershade?
Must love with love share naught but happiness,
Nor make its own the sorrows that oppress
The heart which yields the only joy it knows,
From which the essence of its being flows?
Nay, thus to share thy sorrows but shall be
To add to love a keener ecstasy;
Nor deem thy voice one accent e'er can tell
To pain this bosom—lest it be *farewell*,
For still with thee this heart can know no pain,
And welcome sorrow when we part again."

While thus she spoke proud adoration filled
His throbbing heart, with quickening pulses thrilled,
As in his eyes rose those all holier fires
Which pure affection in the breast inspires,
While thus devotion in her heart displayed
New springs of goodness scarce before betrayed,
From which sweet Faith with gracious hand supplied
Entrancing draughts, thus doubly sanctified.
But when of parting her loved accents spoke,
From his sweet dream of happiness he woke,
And in his heart, as falls a funeral knell,
Broke the dread portence of that word, *farewell.*
Across his face anew pain's shadow crept,
While in his eyes their wonted brightness slept,
As sorrow-filled they sought the neighboring sea,
In deep unquiet, as he made reply.
Then thus he spoke: " My Lolo, could'st thou see
Within my heart its weight of agony,
That from thy side a voice all must obey—
Liberty's death-cry, summons me away,
Would love dare hide what honor's act hath done
From thee e'en still my own, my lovely one,
That for thy sake no slightest cloud should lower
To cast one shadow in this longed for hour.
Whence now I come, beset by tyrant hate,
Gathered, our brothers for the struggle wait;
Wait till our Cuba's foes again shall know
Not unavenged her children's blood shall flow.

For though on freedom treads the oppressor's heel,
Crushing it downward, shall the tyrants feel
For them from freedom's bleeding wrongs shall
    flow
A vengeance deadlier than their hate can know.
Yes, I have dared enlist for liberty
The life which love consecrated to thee,
'Neath whose promptings returned to thee, I bear
My anxious heart, which asks thine own to share
Its sacrifice,—the strength of love alone
Love's faltering purpose can sustain, sweet one.
The midnight passed unknown the shades of fate,
For thee my heart with longing pulses beat,
Whose sweet assurance should impart new life
To brave the perils of th' impending strife.
Then, though 't was death, for thee, my loveliness,
Scaling the rocks which wall the mountain pass
Where lie our band, I sought the neighboring sea,
Whose friendly billows bore me safe to thee."
She heard, yet dared not trust her tongue t' impart
The cry of sorrow echoing in her heart,
As motionless she clung to his embrace,—
Save that along her frame her deep distress
A tremor sent, the coldness of despair
Within her heart, which now was chilling there.
"And is it thus?"—Then shut within her breast,
By sorrow prisoned, her sad accents ceased,
As on his breast she sank,—a drooping flower,

Voiceless beneath that grief which hath but power
To feel, and in its night of woe to see
But the dark image of its agony!
"Nay let not tears bedim thy lustrous eyes,
Nor cloud of sorrow o'er thy beauty rise,
For though night lowers it must pass away,
And oh, what brightness waits returning day
Before the sunlight melts along the main
Its waves must bear me to our band again,
While hope shall guard love's consecrated shrine,
Which sacred charge to it must love resign."

"To hope," she sobbed, "to hope, whose changeful
     ray,
Ever receding, beams but to betray,   .
While still with light delusive it illumes
The mists of sorrow which it ne'er consumes.
But no" (and now in calmer voice she spoke,
Though from her breast its anguished pulses broke
In trembling utterance), "no, our country's need
Must not unanswered to her children plead;
And shall her daughters from that cup once shrink
Which to its dregs her sons so proudly drink?
Go thou, my Pasco, though each hour shall knell
Its wail of sorrow from this sad farewell,
And night returning in each breath shall sigh
The weary reckoning of recurring day
Till thy return. O God, should this be not!"—

And hope shrank, trembling, from that direful
    thought,
As one deep pang of anguish swept her breast
And choked its pulses, trembling into rest.
Amid the flowers he laid her form, and now
Smoothed the dark tresses from her pallid brow,
And with caresses, as o'er he kneeled,
Sought to restore the life which pain congealed,
And through their channels from her heart to bear
The crowding currents which were chilling there!
A spirit-tenderness sought her sweet face,
Soothing each line to placid loveliness;
A beatific calm, like that in death
Which still reflects, though ceased fore'er the breath,
The soul's last, sweetest smile, serenely spread
O'er the all but living features of the dead.
Now raised her eyelids, fringed in mourning hue,
Where tears were trembling, as the early dew
Trembles in beauty, 'neath the paling night,
Ere well the sun dissolves it into light.
On him, half wondering, fixed her saddened eyes,
Where resignation draped love's sympathies,
Which there were gathered, with her sable shade,
For hope deep in the heart's sepulchre laid.

As in his arms he raised her to his side,
Around his neck her own were fondly laid,

While that pure tribute, love's chaste throbbings
   yield,
Upon his lips in lingering fear was sealed.
"Farewell, my Lolo," and his voice betrayed
The deep emotion which his bosom swayed;
"Farewell; the night must to my comrades prove
That Pasco's honor's stronger than his love,
And shame the fear which stings my thought to view,
That to his country Pasco is untrue.

      *   *   *   *

One kiss—another—
               Now alone she stood
Amid the shades of grief's dread solitude,
While in her heart, else lifeless, echoed o'er
Love's anguished accents: "lost for evermore."

VII.

The moon high o'er El Cobre's sombre height
Dispelled the shades of the impending night,
Flooding the vale and towering mountain side
In silvery light. Adown the valley gleamed
In gentle curves, the river's wandering tide,
Till gliding 'twixt a chasmed rock it seemed
To seek repose 'neath the o'ershadowing height,—
Whose frowning brow repelled the soft moonlight,—
As some great serpent winds its weary length

Into the darkness of the cavern's strength.
Weird, ominous, like dread plutonian shades,
High up the mount, o'er glooming crag and pass,
Ranged the dark pines, which the bright, starry
        hosts,
Sentrying the night, seemed watching tremulous!
No sound disturbed the stillness save the cry
Of the lone night-bird, calling plaintively,
With the soft voice, communing with the night,
Of falling water, white in the moonlight,
Which from the mountain sought the river's breast,
And with it mingling, hushed itself to rest.
Far up the height, along a winding pass,
Broad hewn by nature from the mountain's mass,
Now and anon gleamed, 'gainst the darkened
        height
Of rock o'ertowering, the portentous light
Of glist'ning steel, whose momentary gleams
Chilled the soft whiteness of the moon's pale
        beams.
There on the height repose the patriots sought,
Slumbering upon their arms, yet wakeful caught
The voice which told another hour had gone
That cunning Time from friendly Night had won,
As in the mount's defile the sentinel
In cautious utterance said, "Men all is well,"
Then quick again upon the pass he stood,
Courting its shades, as the calm solitude

Of vale and pass he watched with jealous care,—
Ah! who could dream that death was lurking there?

*   *   *   *

VIII.

"And dost thou think the rebel watch can sight
From where thou say'st they hold yon mountain
        height,
The stream below, where shades its breadth half o'er
Yon darkening cliff? There may the farther shore
Alone be reached; too deep the river's bed
Here, where concealed these friendly shades o'er-
        spread,
To ford its depths:—and 'tis a soldier's creed
If men must die, 't is nobler that they bleed;
Then if our foes be they of Yara's fight,
None may be spared who strive for Spain to-night.
But there we cross,—and thou canst lead us on,
As thou hast said, and by a path unknown?"

"I can, my chief; within a gorge it ends,
And thence the way 'neath towering rocks ascends
To a plateau where lie the rebel crew—
The pass is sure—the rest an hour must show!"
"Thou speakest well. Soldiers," he turning, said,—
The dark battalion there beneath the shade
Stood motionless,—

"The enemies of Spain
Keep yonder height, nor dream ere night shall wane
The rocks that now their rebel slumbers keep
Loud shall re-echo with their own death-shriek.
We cross below where yonder rock o'ershades;
Look to your arms; see that no naked blades
A warning bear to traitor eyes, for know
But to their hearts such messengers should go."
Then to the guide: "Pepillo, lead the way;
Now steady—March!" The column moved away
Along the stream, and silently it trod
With measured cadence o'er the yielding sod.
Soon reached the ford, they halted. "Pepillo,
Scan well the height—say, canst thou see the foe?"
"Look thou, my chief, see'st thou that gleam of
    light?
Wait but a moment—now upon the height
Above the fall?"
                "Aye, there—but now 't is gone"—
"Lose not a moment"—
                    "Steady, men, as one,
March!"
        In they moved. Invaded thus, the stream
Plaintively murmured, as in some strange dream
The restless slumberer.
                    —Soon 't was left to rest,
And scarce a ripple trembled on its breast.
Traversed the plain, 'neath the disguising wood

Soon at the mount the halted column stood.
Once more was scanned with stealthy eyes the height;
Once more there glimmered that betraying light,
As the clear moon illumed the pass, till now
Veiled by the shadows from the cliff's dark brow.
Beneath the pines that clothed the mountain side
The chief held whispered council with the guide;
Then at their head, prepared to lead the band,
Pepillo waited for the chief's command,
Who at his side in measured whispers said,
While all stood motionless as are the dead,
"Now comrades, softly; muffle e'en your breath,
Nor let your footsteps tell of coming death.
When reached the gorge, by fours close column keep;
Thence scarce ten paces where the rebels sleep,
Where once again must traitors' bosoms feel
The deadly coldness of the Spaniards' steel."

*　　*　　*　　*

IX.

Along the orient sky the day,
In morning robes of sombre gray,
Crept on apace, as Pasco stood
In turn to guard the solitude
Of the defile and vale below,
Which now the moon—suspended low,
With shadows thronged, that lengthening loomed

Along the glen, slow, weirdly gray,
Like shades of Titan forms away
From their tombs summoned,—on earth doomed
To silence, gathering dark-plumed there,
As if the dying night to bear
To its mysterious sepulchre!

Beneath the soothing breath of morn
His comrades, all fatigued and worn
By marches long and restless sleep,
Now lay, o'ercome, in slumber deep,—
Yet wakeful o'er each weary breast
One thought watched o'er the patriots' rest:
Ah, but for this it had been mad
To trust to slumber all they had
In hope,—from freedom's beckoning star
Which brightly beamed, though distant far!
That thought their land, which to such hearts
A deathless, double life imparts.
An hour had passed, and Pasco stept
Within the pass to where still slept
His comrades, though their eyelids lay
Just closed by sleep's sweet mystery.
He turned the cliff—

                    Then forward sprang,
As on the startled silence rang,
Rebounding with a hundred shocks

From peak to peak of towering rocks,
His carbine's crash—the signal set
Should night unmask her dread alarms,
And they surprised, by foes beset,
No moment find to *call* to arms—
For springing from a neighboring height,
With bayonets glimmering in the light
Of early dawn, he there beheld
The hated foe,—as wildly swelled
Those maddening pulses in his breast
Those feel by tyranny oppressed,
Which know no wilder throb of hate
Than that when face to face they meet
Their Despot's slaves, who crav'n would dare
To bind them with the chains they wear!
Quick as his thought his lead as true,
Struck from the cliff a foeman low;
Nor had the signal failed, as told
A crash of musketry which rolled,
Re-echoing with the thunder's might
From where the patriots held the height,
'Neath which above the crash arose
The death-shriek of a score of foes,
Which from the patriots brought a cry
Of stern, defiant mockery.
Then quick, in fierce reply, out-rang,
As Pasco 'midst his comrades sprang,
A volley from the Spaniard band,

Now closing fast on every hand,
And 'neath its storm of iron hail
Full many a noble patriot fell,
Employing still ere hushed by death,
The accents of his latest breath
In freedom's name, as to her foes
His shout of proud defiance rose.
As sweeps the waves' impetuous might
Against the cliff's opposing height,
Their foam-locks streaming in the storm,
Each like some fierce, demoniac form,
On rushing with resistless force
The strength which seeks to stay their course,
Till backward hurled in turn they lie
Low quivering in their parent sea,
Again to rise—and yet again;
As oft' flung backward to the main,
Yet shivering as they fiercely rush
The rock-firm height they may not crush!
So now, with bayonets set, and hair
Back floating on the troubled air,
No time for aught save steel now left,
Forward the island patriots swept,
Led on,—if aught the brave e'er *lead*,
By Pasco, waving at their head
Their country's flag, full proud to give
Their lives, that its loved cause might live.
Fired by the madly coursing blood
Which swelled each pulse, a frenzying flood,

Upon the hireling foe they dashed
Undaunted, though out-belching flashed,
Full in their course, a withering breath
Of flame-red-tongued, which seethed with death.
Mute as the dead, nor stopped, nor stayed,
With fixèd eyes and jaws close laid;
Each springing where a comrade fell,
There summoned by his last death-yell,
Breathing that atmosphere of hell!
Onward they swept like wave on rock,
Till now, with all resistless shock,
Closing upon the foe, they rushed—
Beneath that shock, recoiling, crushed
Down—down, as many a bosom writhed
Beneath the freezing steel there sheathed;
That lingered not, but quick once more
With tireless vengeance reeked in gore
From breast to breast, congealing there
The currents stagnant 'neath despair,
Till cleft the arm which urged it fell
Low quivering in its purple rill!

High swelled the frightful din of war,
The wild death-shriek; the shivering jar
Of splintering steel; the stifled groan,
Half choked ere breathed; the fitful moan
From life's low pulse; the sabres' clash;
The murd'rous volley, flash on flash;
The locking bayonets, rent apart.

To plunge revengeful in each heart,
As if, imbued with very life,
Conscious they shared their masters' strife!
Now backward forced, scarce half remain,
But step by step—then yet again
Fierce dashing on the wavering foe,
Each laid another Spaniard low,
As sinews straining, hand to hand,
The few still left of that brave band—
Pale as the dead; each forehead set
With beads of cold, congealèd sweat;
Sprang at a foe, defiant still,
In hate which death alone could kill.

Ah! who that awful shock may tell,
When waves of human anger swell
In fierce contention; battling where
Meet livid hate and grim despair;
Who paint that hour of frenzied strife
When passion spares not—asks not life;
Nor thrills to joy's exultant breath
As to the closing cry of death
Forced from the heart wherein the steel
It presses with a savage zeal!

Beset as one of wolves the prey,
O'ermatching numbers kept at bay,
Back forced, contesting foot by foot;
Red-stained from many a streaming cut,
There Pasco, foremost in the fray,

Battled the foe defiantly!
Above his head the flag he held,
One arm but free its folds to shield,
Which wielded with resistless might
His sabre,—busiest in the fight.
Struck from his hands the colors lay.
Forward he dashed: the foe gave way,
Save one more bold who dared contest
His way, and sought from him to wrest
The prize regained, but all in vain—
One more was numbered with the slain!
As up his height he proudly drew,
And fearless scoffed the hated foe.
But the fast ebbing scarlet tide
Down coursing from this breast and side,
Had sapped his life, and his proud cry
Broke in a gasp of agony!
Fast on their victim doomed they press—
Back yielding, till by deep abyss,
From which up-rose a doleful roar,
Like that from waves which beat the shore,
Far distant heard, now Pasco stood
Defiant still—still unsubdued,
While round him, eager for his life,
His foes fast closed.   The torrent's strife,
Deep down the gorge, he heard, and knew
It swept unmeasured depths below,
Nor aught between where hope could trace
For Daring's foot a refuge place!

Then the first fear his bosom knew
Cast o'er his face a pallid hue,
As there commingling curdled stood
Out-starting drops of sweat and blood.
One glance quick sought the foe-kept pass;
Quick one the yawning precipice,
Then with a shout of proud disdain,
A challenge to the arms of Spain!
He turned and down the cañon leaped,
Still grasped the flag so bravely kept;
So nobly borne in life, 't was meet
In death 't should be his winding-sheet.

X.

The struggle o'er, in death's embrace
Each patriot soldier, face to face
There with his foe, sank down to rest,
Undrawn the steel from many a breast.
The sunbeams there that morning played
On many a shattered sabre blade
Still grasped—with strength which, yieldlessly,
Surviving life, seemed to defy
E'en death—by those who, now laid low
Fore'er, there but an hour ago
Opposed them in that deadly strife,
Refusing, as they spared not life !
Still now the scene, which but before
Re-echoed with fierce battle's roar;

And mingling there together flowed
The Patriots' and the Spaniards' blood.
No sign of life was seen save where
The vulture hovering high in air
Amid the sky's ethereal blue,
Looked down upon the scene below.
As they had fall'n, so there they lay
Till Time should hide them in decay;
Nor lived one of that band to tell
How Cuba's valiant children fell!

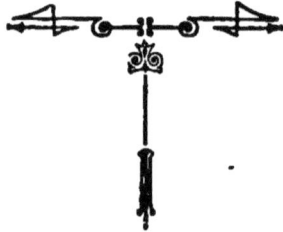

MAY.

A PASTORAL.

"Spreads the fresh verdure of the fields and leads
The dancing Naiads through the dewy meads."
Cowper.

I.

Hail vernal goddess with thy floral train!
Nor from thy praises can my Muse refrain,
As thou, approaching with thy bright-clad throng,
Awak'st the earth to merriment and song.
With loudest praise 't would welcome thee again
As thy swift forces drive back o'er the main
With shafts of sunlight, from the blighted earth,
The ice-shod powers of the frozen North!
It would thy course o'er hill and mead pursue.
As all thou deck'st with robes of richest hue,
And strew'st with flowers whose countless challice
    blooms
Upon the air exhale their sweet perfumes.

Beneath bright skies, fresh-azured from thy hand,
Which smiling bend t' embrace the waiting land,
Adorned by thee, see kindly mother Earth
Invite a-field her children.   Health and Mirth,

(45)

Laughter and joy respond exultantly,
And haste to join thy jocund company,
While on glad wing, upon thy course attend
The plumaged choir called from the summer-land.

Close in thy steps, by sportive Frolic led,
The merry cortege gambols o'er the mead,
While songs of gladness fill the scene around,
Which hill and dale harmoniously resound,
Borne by the swift-winged zephyrs through the air,
Till Joy's full voice reëchoes everywhere!

II.

All beauteous Spring! thou darling of the spheres,
Before whose smile shamed Winter disappears;
His face conceals yet lingers to survey
The glad'ning prospects which thy charms display.
What are thy charms let Nature's self declare
To those who doubting to her courts repair,
Where scenes delightful stretch on every hand,
When thou with beauty spread'st the smiling land.
Thy glory—not the pageantry of kings,
My Muse adoring all enraptured sings;
Not wealth's vain pomp, which partial Fate bestows
Upon the few to mock the many's woes—
Sinking its slaves in luxuries that blind
Till man becomes unfaithful to mankind;
Not thus with thee: with bounty prodigal,
Impartially dost thou dispense to all,

Around the peasant in his lowly cot,
Strewing thy gifts where princes are forgot,
Nor circumscribed 'mong all earth's kind appears
The meanest being but thy riches shares!

And thus thy hands e'en o'er the lonely dead,
Richest of flowers with lavish kindness spread,
Whose blossoms laden with most rare perfume,
Attest thy memory of the silent tomb.
There where the cherished of our hearts repose
When reached that bourne where life's tired foot-
        steps close
Beneath o'er-bending shades they brightly bloom,
Tinting the deepening shadows of the tomb,
By thee from earth, 'neath winter's blight there laid,
Raised to new life—fit emblems of the dead.
There, like sweet guardian angels they appear,
Breathing rich incense on the hallowed air
And, spirit-voiced, in language love may know,
Commune with us of those who sleep below,
While their pure symbols to fond memory give
The sweet assurance that they ever live.

But still the glories of thy work I sing,
O ever beauteous, ever friendly Spring!
Amid thy scenes delighted still I stray,
And all thy charms with fondest joy survey.
O'er hill and dale behold the forests bare,
The foremost subject of thy generous care,

To thee out-stretching their denuded arms,
Impatient for the robes and floral charms
Thou bringest them—their shivering limbs long bare
To hostile winter's rough and frigid air,
Till verdure clad, they stand magnificent:
Of thy great work the grandest monument!

III.

As the fresh Morn, pluming her wings of light,
Suffused with beauty takes her joyous flight
From the blue arch that holds the orient sky,
Which her bright wings with roseate tints supply:
When the first beams of the approaching day
With aureate splendor gild earth, sky, and sea,—
That tranquil hour which Contemplation loves,
When Nature from her dewy slumber moves,—
How sweet to wander o'er the smiling fields,
And breathe the fragrance Nature's garden yields,
As, one by one, the waking songsters raise
From hedge and branch their grateful matin lays,
With tuneful brooks and music-whispering trees,
Greeting the morn with sweetest symphonies.
There crowning all in the delightful scene,
The sun with gold floods earth's imperial green,
As on the view come forth in glorious birth
Unnumbered flowers to deck their mother earth,
Till field and forest, bathed in radiant light
Stand forth all beauteous—rapturing the sight,
While wakened Nature in glad concert sings,

By warblers led, who with applauding wings,
Softly accordant, swell the praiseful hymn
Which heavenward rises, incensed by perfume!

High 'mid the blue the lark pours his glad song,
And hurrying by the swallow sweeps along
Glancing aside or as she upward springs
Flashes the sunbeams from her lightning wings.
The faithful redbreast, first of all the year,
Sings to its mate in numbers softly clear,
And gives good-morrow to the whistling thrush,
Who sends his greeting from a neighboring bush.
Along the meads brooks babble as they run,
O'er pebbles irridescent 'neath the sun,
With smiles for every flower and every blade
Which their glad course attend through wood and
        glade,
Along their marge the clustering cresses grow
Fringing the banks, where new-born violets blow.
Whence thick a-field, gilding the velvet mead,
The regal king-cups their gold livery spread,
While everywhere o'er field and woodland sway
In balmy breezes the sweet flowers of May.
Upon some mount that overlooks the mead
Reclined, the view commanding wood and glade,
Whence to the hills the freshly verdured ground
In graceful undulations spreads around,
How rapturous on each lovely scene to dwell
And, yielding to sweet Meditation's spell,

To contemplate Nature's stupendous scheme,
Wondrous creation of a Power supreme!
On every hand some lesson man may learn,
In every flower some sacred truth discern,
In beauty shown, fresh from the source of all
Given to man by wisdom bountiful.
View 'mid sharp thorns the rose her beauty wears,
E'en as the thorn the sweetest blossoms bears;
Mark the meek violet, and the giant tree,
Share His regard, each in required degree,
All eloquent, His high munificence
Proclaim, and show impartial Providence!

The day is done—and evening gently veils
In violet light the hills; the wooded dales
In deeper tints, as 'neath the western dome
The twilight lingers till the stars be come.
The lowing herd slow homeward wends its way;
Each drowsy member following o'er the lea—
Loitering a moment at the wayside stream
On which the last faint flecks of daylight gleam.

Amid the wood, sings modest Philomel;
Upon the silence her love madrigal
As sweetly falling as the tinkling rill
Heard through the midnight when all else is still.
Softly quick Echo, wakened at the strain,
Replies accordant to the sweet refrain

From secret haunts which none but wood-nymphs
    know,
Save the Enchantress of the lunar bow.
Soon dewy showers disturb the evening lay,
And Philomela's warblings die away,
As with her Echo sinks into repose,
And silence o'er the earth her mantle throws.

Thou God of Life, all-wise, all-bountiful!
Eternal One! as thou art source of all
The riches which the ladened Seasons bear
To fill the Earth with beauty everywhere,
The power—the glory which my grateful theme
Would celebrate unto Thy sacred name
Alone belong, as the revolving spheres
With countless tongues, along the rolling years,
Ceaseless proclaim!   Still ever be it mine
To swell the praises of Thy power divine;
To know Thee ever as Thou dost reveal
Thyself in Nature, where *Invisible*
Doth name Thee not, Almighty One! for there
In love and power configured Thou dost appear!

THE OLD SEXTON'S CHRISTMAS DREAM.

I.

'Tis Christmas eve, and a cold clear night,
And the earth is filled with the white moon-light,
Which falls through the frosty air from on high,
From the crystal blue of a winter's sky,
And glistening rests on the drifted snow,
And gleams on the half-iced stream below;
And the slumbering earth, robed in white, arrays
With multitudinous diamond sprays,
By the Frost-king there unradiant strewn,
Till illumed by the white-fire touch of the moon.

II.

Round the mountain's base the river glides,
'Neath the shadowy pine on its rugged sides,
And creeps through the vale by the evergreen shade;
By the fringing willows, all leafless made;
By the hazel-copse, by the ice-bound wheel
Of the moated, long unbusy mill,
And into the quiet burg hard by,
Whose quaint tile roofs sharply rise on high,
Then onward flows to the distant wood,
Where its voice alone stirs the solitude.

(52)

III.

The village church caps a neighboring hill,
O'ergrown with ivy and tufted moss,
'Neath giant poplars weirdly still,
Which a shadowy net-work weave across
The snow's white folds on roof and tower,
(There deftly spread as by magic power);
While above gleams the spire with its cross on
high,
Set 'mid the brilliants that fill the sky.

IV.

From the gothic windows a dim light creeps
Through the colored panes, and softly glows
On the whitened sills, where it restless sleeps,
Or steals o'er the clustering moss that grows
On mullion and transom and eaves above,
(By lacing ivy there interwove);
Then fades within—to appear again
Softly tinting the many-colored pane.

V.

Old Kasper, the sexton, had wrought within
As the midnight hour crept on apace,
With clusters of holly and evergreen
Adorning the walls of the holy place,
Till weary grown; yet with heart aglow
As he thinks of the morrow's eve, and how
The children, with faces alight, will press

Round the Christmas tree in its loveliness.
Now a little rest, as he croons a hymn,
He seeks in a cushioned sconce, the while
In the flickering light, growing yet more dim,
O'erscanning the drapings in chancel and aisle;
And reclining thus—soothed the tired sight
'Neath cradling shadows that flit and creep,—
Unconscious he drifts 'neath the trance of night
And the mind, flower-wise, folds itself in sleep.

VI.

'Tis the Elfin band who all silently
Weave the web of sleep, have him captive ta'en
And laid 'neath the spell of their sorcery
They bind him tight with their silken chain,
And in shadowy folds, which they weave from night,
They muffle him close for their mystic flight.

'Tis the potent watch of the Elfin reign,
And they gather fast on every hand,
And soon at their visored chief's command
Is their captive borne to their bright domain,
To the golden scenes of the vision-land.
Swift as thought its enchanted bounds they pass
And its brilliance breaks 'neath the bluest height
Of a fairyland bathed in roseate light,
Filled with throngs of its airy populace.
And they move through grottos with jewels bright,
Glittering many-hued in the rich rose-light,

That steals within, with the perfumed air,
From the flower-filled dells of the mystic sphere,
Half seen beyond, 'twixt the arches high,
Whence comes the sound of festivity.

VII.

The shadowy veil from the captive falls
And his bonds change to garlands of blossoms rare,
And they onward move as when pleasure calls
And gladness and beauty is everywhere.
And thus to the royal court they come;
Reared on tinted marbles its crystal dome,
Round circling in graceful colonnades,
With fountains between, and emblossomed shades,
And in the midst on an ivory throne,
(Its seat irridescent opal stone),
Sits the Fairy-Queen robed in lily white,
And crowned with a circlet of diamond light.

VIII.

On every side 'neath her gracious smile
Her people the festive hours beguile
In merry round, while on busy wing
Some richest fruits to the banquet bring.
For in fairy realm,—as proclaims the scene
With its joy, good cheer and emblems green
Speaking grateful praise,—'tis a time of feast
And thanksgiving for a danger past

To a noble king who freed their land
From a giant grim, and on every hand
Rarest fruits are spread, and glad heralds call
Fairyland to the royal festival.

IX.

They gather fast from glade and grot,
Elves and sylvan sprites and butterfly fays,
Their little forms decked in textures wrought
From flowers and broidered with gossamer rays,
And they join in the bright festivities,
Till the scene with their bouyant gladness rings,
While the air is filled with sweet harmonies
From their tinkling spangles and tuneful wings.

X.

But all is hushed ; for the fairy-queen
Stands forth, and surveying with gracious mien
The throngs which gallery and court-ways fill,
Thus in accents clear speaks the sovereign will :—
" Our much-loved people, most glad are we
To welcome you all to our royal fête,
On this festal day when the memory
Of our Champion-King we celebrate.
Throughout the bounds of our goodly State
To share our joy we have called you here,
And your presence with loving heart we greet,
The humblest alike with our highest peer.

So all strangers sojourning in our domain,
Have we bidden come—alike welcome all,
For all hearts should meet on love's equal plane
This day of love's grateful festival.

"To-day, as he whom we honour came
Of his own free will and kingly grace
To save our realm, love alone should claim
Our hearts and therein all else displace,
While each for the other's happiness
Gives foremost thought, as true love e'er will,
And so shall the hours most joyous pass
And goodness her highest charge fulfill.
For the choice first-fruits which our people bring,
As their custom 'tis from year to year,
An oblation to our most honoured king,
We yield due thanks.   We ourselves shall bear
Your offerings to him whom we all revere,
For in honouring him most honour we
Ourselves and the State we hold most dear,
Which to him proudly yields its fealty.

" And now let the feast proceed.   Let all
In our joy and good cheer participate,
While the Dance and Song in glad carnival
Rule the hour.   Let each present emulate
The next in mirth; let our banquet hall
With rejoicings loud reverberate;

While all hearts are linked in a chain of love
That not fate nor the tides of years can move."

XI.

The Sovereign ceased.   A round of glad acclaim
And greetings followed, till the sound did seem
To fill the air, yet soft as music is
Of trebles sweet in gentlest harmonies.
Poised o'er the throne or gliding on swift wing
The fays of air moved gaily—scattering
About their Queen rare floral sweets, whose blooms
Imbued the air with delicate perfumes.

XII.

Throughout, the dwellers in this mystic sphere
Greeted with joy their stranger visitor,
Tendering rich fruits where'er he chanced to pass,
As curtsying low with smiles and airy grace,
Or strewing blossoms as he moved along
Entranced with wonder 'mid the Fairy throng ;
Wondering the while that so much beauty dwelt
So close to earth, unknown—unguessed—unfelt.

*   *   *   *

XIII.

So sped the hours—how swiftly do they fly
When only gladness bears them company ;
When the rapt soul is moved by joy alone
And recollection of all else is gone ;
So sped the hours,—enchanting as they passed,

Sparkling with beauty all too bright to last.

          *   *   *   *

And now appeared high 'mid the luminous air,
Flashing fresh beams of beauty everywhere.
A form refulgent ; than all else more bright
Bathing the scene in wonder-working light.
Investing all ; each ray a shaft of flame,
In might increasing as it grandly came,
Till it did seem as its full glory filled
The scene, (quick at the radiant advent stilled
To breathless calm) all in its strength to hold
And to transfigure into shimmering gold.
The ambient blue dissolved ; a tremulous glow
Of opal splendor flooded all below,
As countless hues there glittering but before,
Slow fading from the view, were seen no more.
Yet though bereft of color still remained
Each form and outline in the vision-land,
But silent now and motionless—a sight
Of phantom pictures melting into light.
Then 'neath its power, soon all potential grown,
The fairy realm ; its populace, the throne
To formless light were fused—

                        And Kasper woke
As on his face, through the church windows, broke
The rising sun ; the sun of Christmas day
Flooding the earth with its resplendent ray.

CHATTERTON.

———

Inspire, O Muse, the sadd'ning theme I raise
To one who loved thy presence,—sang thy praise
In sweetest voice of all thy minstrel choir
From the first hour his fingers swept the lyre
Received from thee,—its dulcet strings supplied
From silver in that fire purified
Which in the temple of thy sacred hill,
Though now but smouldering, warms thy altar still.
Inspire my theme: a theme adorned to grace
The sweetest song, the noblest minstrel's lays,
To one whose lyre, so rich its numbers came,
Shed a new glory on thy sacred name.
A heaven-born spirit which from its bright sphere
Wandering to earth, lingered a little here
To sing the songs which it had known before
With kindred spirits on the Elysian shore,—
Earth's tongue in their celestial harmonies
Re-echoing here the music of the skies!

(60)

Sweet bard! how bright thy sun of promise rose,
Yet oh, what shadows gathered toward the close,
And ere it reached the height of life's noon-day
Fore'er in darkness quenched its wondrous ray.
How bright that sun, behold where passed its light
Its brilliance gl ows athwart obstruction's night,
And adds new life to that immortal flame
Whose sacred fires illume the heights of Fame.

As lesser spheres a symmetry do show
As truly perfect as the greater, so
The narrowed circle of thy life not less
Perfection showèd for its littleness,
Where, like the planet with the belt of light,
Thy star of Genius blazed along the height
Of fame unique; and though so quickly gone,
Gave forth a glory which was all thine own.
Of all mankind the Muse did e'er endow
'Twas thine alone mature in youth to know.
"The gift divine," wherein thou didst display—
An inspiration but revealed in thee,
With genius, knowledge; knowledge e'en earth's
    Seers
Amazed beheld—to all the work of years !

Amid the quiet of primeval woods,
Where the sweet voices of its solitudes
Contentment breathed, the brook, the meek-faced
    flower,
The grateful songster, and in night's still hour

The stars were thy sweet loves, still sought by thee
With more than fondest lover's constancy,
Drawn to their chasteness by that force that gives
To love to seek its own correlatives.
With the eternal hills : the great, deep sea
Familiar didst thou commune ; they to thee
Were but as loved companions.   With dread voice
The Tempest, robed in night, earth, sea and skies
Stirring to strife—as through the trembling air,
Hurling its bolts it swept, its course the glare
Of the fierce lightnings 'luming,—was to thee
A sight which gave thy soul supremacy
Of joy, as with the Storm-king's awful form
Attendant rode thy spirit on the storm !

Thy faithful heart,—e'en as the clinging vine
Struck by the worm, round its loved ones did twine
Its richest offerings, yielding sweetest breath
E'en while below cankered the worm of death.
Thy love its rich warm soil ; its only air
Draughts humid 'neath the cold mists of despair ;
Its only light, hope's distant, dying ray,
A spark expiring in eternal day !

Relentless fate, inexplicable doom !
Which thus consigned thy genius to the tomb,
And swept thy hopes ; thy promise richly fair
Into the grave to sleep forever there,
Nor let thee know in life's resigning breath
The kindred voice that soothes the pain of death.

Then in thy mind bright scenes forever past,
Upon thy soul distracting shadows cast,
'To make thine anguish still but deeper grow,
Till thou hadst supped the very dregs of woe ;
While—as the lightning's momentary flight
Illumes the clouds, encumbering the night,
And breaks the darkness of the midnight sky
But to increase its black intensity,—
Memories of home within thy hapless breast
Flashed through despair's thick cloud that round
    thee pressed,
Which in their brightness served but to illume
And show how dark the shadows of the tomb,
And, passed away, in thy distracted mind,
Left a dread darkness doubly black behind.

Insatiate Pride ! beneath thy direful sway,
Thou scourge of earth, thou subtle votary
Of Death ! of Genius all thou mayst o'ercome,
How oft hath sought the silence of the tomb.
Youth, Beauty, Worth, earth's mightiest thy prey ;
O'erthrown by thee see Nations in decay,
Of which thou'st left,—of Genius, Nations all,
But monuments to show how great their fall.
Serpent-like, coiled within that hapless breast,
Implacable ! 'Twas thou his life oppressed ;
With lying tongue on to destruction, stilled
The voice of reason, thou his steps beguiled,

Then e'en when most thou promised, did betray
To death the victim of thy perfidy.
And thou, O World ! in thy cold selfishness,
Witnessed the victim fall, yet to distress,
Borne e'en that thou might'st greater riches know,
Brought not relief, nay, dealt the final blow
Which all of genius death hath power to bind,
To the dark precincts of the tomb confined.

Is it for this the Muse her riches gives ;
Is it for this that patient Genius strives
Earth's unseen things of beauty to reveal
From secret places gleaned with tireless zeal,—
To live the drudge of penury and care ;
The dupe of hope ; the victim of despair ;
The world's cold incredulity to brave ;
To sink forgotten to a timeless grave,
That those may share a wealth which else must lie
Buried in Nature's sealed infinity,
Who while they scruple not the fruits t' enjoy,
Ungrateful coldly pass the laborer by.

May shame o'erwhelm thee, Selfishness ! when on
The tomb that holds the dust of Chatterton
Thou look'st.   Thou Pride, should'st thou per-
        chance there too
Resort, may'st thou remorseful sorrow know,
While humbled ye within your hearts confess,
Else dumb, how less ye are than littleness !

ON THE INDIAN OCEAN.

One summer's day, beside the murmuring sea,
Stretched on the beach, I slept, and dreamed I saw
A noble ship, which, out upon the deep,
Moved proudly o'er the waters toward the east.
Calm as a mountain lake the ocean lay
Beneath the brightness of a tropic sun,
Yet did it seem as if the sultry air
Of summer's heated breath upon its breast
Oppressive lay, and in its mighty heart,
Deep down, disturbed its slumbering forces—stirred
To restless throbbings, as its bosom swelled
In slow pulsation, and then sank away
In strange disquietude.   Encircling, arched
Sublimely o'er the azure vault of heaven,
Upon whose royal height enthronèd sat
The god of day, in dazzling glory robed.
O'er the still depths the ship majestic moved,
As sportively she scattered with her prow,
About her path,—all glittering in the sun,
Unnumbered brilliants of unnumbered hues,
Which she did gather from the emerald deep,
While from her rolled upon the drowsy air

A long, dark line of fume, which sought the haze
Of roseate tint, far in the glimmering distance.
Upon her decks the "toilers of the sea,"
Sun-browned in service, each his duty sought,
While in the rigging some the useless sail
With busy fingers folded to the yards,
All merry-hearted singing as they wrought.
Beneath an awning shading from the sun
Reclined the ocean voyagers, and there
Upon the air all merrily arose
The careless laugh, the voice of happiness,
And busy tongues of little ones at play.
Beauty and Youth with faces bright, illumed
With love and hope, and Age with its sweet smile,
In happiest intercourse assembled were.
Others apart from those thus grouped about
Sought to beguile in quicker pace away,
The lingering hours of the hot summer's day
With tales of Fancy's painting; some o'ercome
By its soporous breath in slumber lay,
While here and there one o'er the bulwarks leaned
In listless dreamings, gazing o'er the wave.
Aside were two: one Beauty's prototype
Set in a frame of fairest loveliness;
The other Beauty's proud defender—Youth
From Nature's sturdier, bolder model, man.
As silvery clouds in fleecy softness veil
The chasteness of the virgin summer moon,

Here white attire, in sweet abandon, draped
Her lovely form—in nameless grace composed,
As she, reclined beside him whom she loved,
Gave ear attent, as he read to her thought;
Read of some sorrow, as expression told,
Moulding her face to sweet solicitude—
Of holy sympathy, throned in the heart,
The superscription.   So her lustrous eyes,—
Liquidly brilliant as the glist'ning dew
Upon the new-blown, trembling violet,—
Pearled in warm tears, did each emotion glass,
Which that sad tale awoke within her heart
But this was passed, and like the sun's fresh glow
Of heat and light when April showers are o'er,
With a soft brightness beamed her tear-damped
    eyes,
Resting on him who, ceased, in their sweet depths
Poured from his own love's warm responsive rays.

*   *   *   *

The scene was changed: upon a rock-bound coast
I stood; darkness had gathered over all.
'Gainst the dark sea high loomed the walling cliffs
Amid the starlit air, their towering fronts
Stern frowning, om'nous, warders of the deep,
Robed in the sombre livery of Night.
About their caverned base lamentingly
The troubled waters tossed, 'neath the weird wind,
Which to the night distressfully complained,

In wild and fitful voice.   Higher it rose
And 'neath it soon high swelled and fiercely lashed
The surge in angry clamor 'gainst the cliffs,
While black impenetrable clouds rolled o'er,
Piled mass on mass, high 'mid the thickening air,
And quickly curtained with their darkened folds
The ebon vault of heaven, an hour before
Whence countless stars looked down upon the sea.
Far distant, from its cloud-built battlement,
Rending night's pall, the wakened lightning pierced
With gleaming shaft the bosom of the deep!
Responsive to the Storm-king's awful voice,
Deep-swelling from afar; then opened fast
The many portals of the walling clouds,
Piled up the vaulted height, to passage give
The spirits of the tempest.   Issuing forth,
They, riding on the winds, did fiercely urge
The elements to strife, most clamorous
Where lightning-led they ranged the watery waste,
Which, thus illumined, its waves dark, serpentine,
Revealed, high surging in encounter wild,
Like huge leviathans in fury met
Fiercely contending.   Now above the roar
Of the loud sea the deepening thunder rose—
And died away upon the wind.   Anon
From the dark zenith of the firmament,
In louder voice its angry mutterings broke,
And rolling downward burst into a crash!
Then every cloud, in emulation fierce,

Thundered reply, rending the trembling air,
As through the ambient darkness, inky grown,
Each gave defiant challenge to the night,
And hushed the mighty roaring of the sea.
Flaming, the lightnings, red-tongued, lick the waves,
Which heavenward madly reared their mammoth
    forms,
Till, by the tempest struck, back hurled they plunged
With roars defiant to their surging depths.
Out on the sea, lit by the lightnings' glare,
Flash following flash in wild velocity,
A ship swept on before the tempest's strength,
Rose with the maddened waves, sank as they sank,
Then in the hadean darkness disappeared.

        *   *   *   *   *

The fulmines of the storm were spent, though still
The forces of the winds swept to the cliffs,
Resistless in their might, hurling the waves,
To fury lashed, 'gainst their black adamant,
As if back summoned to their cavern strengths,
Rebellious they in fierce resentment raged.
The broken clouds now hurried o'er the sky,
And laid their shattered masses 'neath the arch
Which marks the southern limits of the heavens,
Their serrate summits by the moon illumed,
Which now released, in mellow brilliancy
Flooded the waves, to very mountains grown.

There, laboring o'er their heights, the doomed ship
Rose, mastless, tottered on their giant crests,
Then headlong plunged to their abyssmal depths,
But rose not up again.—The waves rolled o'er
Inexorable—

          *   *   *   *   *

          From my sleep I woke;
Still murmuring, in the sunset lay the sea.

QUAND MÊME.

———

Once more by the old window with the fragrant
    eglantine,
As of old its sweetness breathing,—now o'ergrown
    with columbine,
Two years this June we parted at this very sunset
    time:
I scarce can realize that since I've been in many a
    clime,
So natural the dear old scene, for though the years
    since gone
Have shown me many beauteous scenes this held my
    heart alone.
And that's the old-time *abendlied*, so loved, which
    now you play,
Whose voice, like some sweet spirit, through the past
    has followed me
In all my wanderings, and when most alone 't was
    sure to come,
And fill me with the deep longings for the then far
    distant home.
Its sad, sweet strain recalls to me the chant of
    vesper bells

(71)

Once heard upon the stillness from a cloister's
    wooded hills,
As close along the Spanish coast one summer's eve
    we bore,
When all was silent save the waves upon the neigh-
    boring shore.
Now heard once more, here at your side, its ne'er
    forgotten strain
Awakes sweet recollections, intermingling joy and
    pain—
Throbbings of joy that sweetly thrill, by busy Mem-
    ory brought,
Then sadly tremble into rest struck by the chill of
    thought,
As fast on recollection comes each well remembered
    scene,
Which now—sweet picture of the past!—but show
    what might have been;
And these alone remain to me of all that happy
    time,
In the heart's darkened chamber hung, draped in
    memoriam.
There might have been no shadows,—if love may
    dare surmise
From the old light which timidly has crept into your
    eyes;
The same that kindled in my heart the flame love
    may inspire,

Which, like watch-lamps in holy fanes, proves but
    memorial fire,
E'er since, when blinder than our hearts,we parted
    hastily
In wounded pride, and I became a wanderer on
    the sea.
It was beside this gate I stood, two summers now
    ago,
And heard you play that melody, which since I've
    cherished so,—
The day I met you—then my love woke to its
    sweet refrain,
And its harmony with silver chords wove round
    my heart a chain,
Which though 'tis rent asunder recollection now
    displays
Its scattered links, which still reflect the scenes of
    happier days;
And with it came an image, then enshrined within
    my heart,
Where it must ever rest undimmed till life there-
    from depart.
Your faithful heart remembers still for though you
    answer not,
That tear now trembling on your cheek shows that
    the springs of thought
Have been disturbed by memory, and thus o'er-
    flowing rise,—

And what a lovely channel have they chosen in
    your eyes.
How changed seems all since last we strolled along
    the old-time way;—
And this is the last meeting we may know for
    many a day,
For I go from here to-morrow, I can scarcely tell
    you where,
I do not know which way myself, in truth I little
    care
But I dare not trust my heart to see another hold
    its shrine,
Which love, denying every claim, e'en now would
    not resign.
But honor binds and points the way love may not
    choose but take;
That way I go, and so good-by—forever for your
    sake.

*   *   *   *

How like lamenting spirits, sigh the trees that
    shade the dead,
Here in the quaint old church-yard, in summer's
    last tints clad,
Where—five years passed, once more returned, I
    look out on the sea,
From the wooded hill-side where she sleeps who
    was so dear to me.

The waves break sadly as I've heard them break
    in many a clime—
Like memories which unceasing fall along the
    shores of time,
And the droning bee hums idly by in the sultry
    August noon,
Lingering to sip from weary flowers which 'neath
    the still heat swoon.
White-winged a solitary ship far out upon the sea,
Reflects the noon-day sunlight, soon o'erclouded,
    and to me
This seems a fitting image of the lot I bear this
    day:
Alone on life's broad ocean, and the sunlight passed
    away,
And o'er its havenless expanse my bark of life must
    bear,
O'ershadowed by those memories which must ever
    darken there.

Thus hope's delusive star how oft in sorrow's night
    declines,
And to dark disappointment's shades our happiness
    consigns;
Yet can the image which awoke that hope ne'er fade
    away—
Embalmed in the heart's sepulchre, from "feeling's
    dull decay."

SONNETS.

A NIGHT IN JUNE.

The deep blue firmament begemmed with light
Bending o'er earth, like love o'er slumbering love;
The spirit *Peace*, descending from above,
Hushing all things to silence as the night
Comes solemnly.   Still as in gentlest flight
The breath of unseen wings, soft zephyrs stray
Among the sleeping flowers, and steal away
Their hearts' perfumes.   Amid the sparkling height
The beetle drones, or falls the night-bird's cry
While insect bands their minim notes attune
On every side—
                  Anon the orient sky
Dissolves in light as the round, silver moon
Sails up the blue in queenly majesty,
The crowning glory of a night in June.

INRI*.

When on the cross hung man's high sacrifice,
  Death near approached his work to execute,
  Awe-struck recoiled, in fear irresolute
His office on his King to exercise.
Then bowing to his breast his head, the Christ
  Made sign to the Implacable, that he,
  Without regard to right of sovereignty,
Should claim the sacrifice at which was priced
Man's sin.   Then did th' Inexorable strike—
  The fearful Sun to darkness paling fled;
  Earth trembling shrank to night's embrace, the
    dead
E'en by that deed of their dread prince made quick
Did him defy—he had forever spent
His power in striking the Omnipotent!

---

*From the French of an unknown author of the seventeenth century; con-
tained in a little poem entitled "La Mort du Christ," which was found in-
scribed upon the principal gate of the cemetery which formerly surrounded
the Church of Sainte Trinité, in Cherbourg.

MUSIC.

—

Come, muse Divine, naught like thy strains compose
    The longing heart, nor there can charm to rest
Its discontent, yet oh, what peace it knows
    When by thy entrancing presence 't is possessed!
E'en as a bird at the first dawn of day
Sought by its mate, joins it and soars away
    Through sun-flushed fields of azure, circling round
High 'mid the blue where spirit joys abound,
My soul solicitous, at thy behest,
    To thy loved realm enraptured wings its flight,
    Led on by thee there lingering with delight;
Soaring aloft—or cradled into rest.
All other joys the passions but control,
'T is thou alone canst reach the inmost soul!

TO-MORROW.

Farewell till flowers return.   Ah, could we know
  The darkness of that said fore'er 't would seem
  Thus marked but as the shadow of a dream;
A transitory cloud ordained to show
How full the light beyond.   Lo now, though far
  To love, Time's darkened corridors between
  Its brightness falls, as through some dark aisle
    seen
The light of day, and thitherto Hope's star
Shall guide the steps of Faith.   So e'en with joy
  May we regard such shadows which Time's flight
  Resolves to pillars of enduring light,
Traced with sweet memories of fond constancy,
Which ever in the after years shall prove
The dearest of all records dear to love!

SOLITUDE.

'Tis sweet at eve to wander by the shore
  And watch the restless waters of the deep,
  As the night winds across its bosom sweep,
Blending their strange complainings with its roar!
'Tis sweet to linger by the shadowy wood
  As, phantom-like, the soft moonlight there creeps,
  Where, 'neath the sentrying stars, tired Nature
      sleeps
And Silence sits enthroned in Solitude!
Such scenes a deep, mysterious pleasure bear,
  And wake a prescient spirit in the breast,
  Timid of day, which from a vague unrest
Finds glad relief raptly communing there
With spirit voices from far spheres which tell
Of distant worlds, to sense invisible!

MEDITATION.

In that still hour when the declining day
   Along the sky fades tranquilly away,
When o'er the earth the glimmering twilight creeps,
   All voices hushing as dear Nature sleeps,
In solitude, naught save the symphony
   Of ocean heard, 'tis sweet to seek thy charms,
   Where naught ignoble the glad soul alarms,
As rapturously it yields itself to thee.
Silent thou art, thy silence eloquence,
   Raising the soul to its inherent life,
Which, casting off its mortal instruments,
   Soars far beyond earth's narrow scene of strife,
And, led by thee, views that immortal state
In which it too shall soon participate!

VENICE.

How doth thy name conjure th' historic past,
  Queen of the Isles; once of the East supreme!
  How to thy courts the proudest Nations came
And at thy feet their richest tribute cast.
Most valiant then thy sons, and thy domains
  Far-reaching as the waves thy galleons cleft;
  Then Venice Victrix! Now apart, bereft;
Of all thy greatness but a name remains!
Thy galleons gone—thy banners sadly furled;
  Still, bride of Ocean, though as queen discrowned,
  'Neath bluest heavens, 'mid beryl seas thou'rt
      throned,
Unique among the marvels of the world!
  Thy glory marked, forever now resigned,
  Tears dim the eyes and wonder fills the mind.

STANZAS.

LOVE AND DIGNITY.

It was June; in a vale, as the day was declining,
  Near a lakelet rose-hued by the soft, waning
    light,
Stately Dignity walked, in the silence resigning
  His thought to those scenes which most gladdened
    his sight.

Not far had he gone when he heard a deep
    sighing
  Which came from a cluster of roses near by,
And great his surprise when among them espying
  The little god Cupid,—who'd uttered the sigh.

On his arm he reclined, with a rose in his fingers,
  From which he was plucking its petals away,
And as a bright star on a cloud's summit lingers,
  . A tremulous tear on his dark lashes lay.

"And what has disturbed you?" asked Dignity,
    kindly.
Cupid started, and fluttered his wings in dismay,
But feared, in the presence he found himself, blindly
    To follow his feelings and scamper away.

He made no reply; simply pointed before him
    Where an arrow lay broken,—the source of his
      woe,
As he bit those sweet lips for which mankind adore
    him,
    And patted his bare little leg with his bow!

"Indeed, and is that it? Just as I expected;
    'T would seem you've not done as instructed "—
      "'T is true,"—
"Precisely, now had you done as I directed "—
    "You would say I'd not had this misfortune to
      rue."

"This once," Love continued, "good Dignity spare
    me,"
Looking up in his face with a coy, suasive smile,
"And come here to-morrow at this hour, and hear me
    Recount my success with proud Beauty mean-
      while."

"Most gladly I will, so good-night, but remember!"
"Never fear," Love replied, with glance roguishly
    bright,
Then with wings rustling softly, as leaves 'neath a
    zephyr,
He rose on a sunbeam and passed out of sight.

*   *   *   *

Next eve to the vale, ere the sun had ceased shining,
    Came Dignity,—'t was one he long had loved
    best,—
And there, on a bed of rich blossoms reclining,
    He beheld Beauty fondling a rose at her breast.

Quick, with rapturing pulsation, his heart beat, but
    hearing
    A sound as of Love's half-suppressed voice near
    by,
He concealed his emotion, then to her appearing,
    He approached, as upon him she smiled gra-
    ciously.

Love had led her hither, and now near her hiding,
    'Mid the blossom-flaked foliage, as Dignity came
He sped a bright arrow, fire-tipped, which dividing
    His heart, kindled there its wild, exquisite flame!

Thus struck, before Beauty he fell, to her pleaded
  To draw from his bosom the still flaming dart;
She, while soothing the wound, saw but Love e'er
      could heal it,
  The arrow was buried so deep in his heart!

Then in flight Cupid cried, " Dignity, I regret to
  Have *missed* you, as now I've no time to wait, for
My quiver is empty.   I did not forget you,
  You see. Now I'm off for a few arrows more!"

Soon though passed out of sight, in soft, dulcet
      numbers
  His voice lingered still, urging his sweet decree,
While the flowers his warm wings had waked from
      their slumbers,
    On the whispering air shed their sweets wan-
      tonly!

Soon 't was clear from the manner of Beauty in
      pressing
  Her hand 'gainst her heart, quickly palpitating,
Love had there sent an arrow,—the rogue when
      professing
    His quiver unstocked, had his darts 'neath his
      wing.

THE GLADIATOR.

The following lines are a *free* translation from the French of Chênedollé (1769–1833), and are presented as of interest by reason of being substantially identical, as will at once be observed, with those so universally known and justly ad. mired of Lord Byron on the same subject, occurring in "Childe Harold." Unfortunately for his French contemporary, it has been incontestibly established that "our author" spoke first by two years.

Spurned, bleeding; victim of a barbarous lust—
   Imperial Rome's! the gladiator falls
   On the arena homicidal, there
In calm repose yielding himself to death.

Low drooped upon his arm, within his heart
   He concentrates his residue of strength;
   *Consents to death, yet conquers agony,**
While dauntless still he braves the Roman foe.

---

*"Il consent à la mort, domptant l'agonie."

Fast fails his strength, and lower sinks his head;
  He feels his life depart. The drops of blood
  Which he beholds calmly and fearless fall,
From his torn side more slowly now descend.

Far from this scene of horror are his thoughts,
  To his loved home alone they fondly turn,
  Where 'neath his roof, beside the Danube's shore
Affection sees his darling infant ones.

Them by their mother's knee he there beholds,
  While in a spectacle inhuman he
  Expiring lies, before an alien race,
Butchered to amuse the Roman populace!

Now o'er his face death's pallid hue is spread;
  He dies, yet ne'er surrendering once to fear,
  While with disdain the shouts prolonged he hears
That hail the victor—guilty of his blood!

Oh, bloody deed!—dare man thus outrage man?
  Rise ye, ye fierce barbarians of the north!
  Speed to revenge your sons' ignoble death;
Quick, lest Rome still finds pleasure in your blood!

HIS REPLY

TO "HER LETTER."

———

I was resting beneath the old pine tree,
But an hour from the mines—tired out—
Alone—worse than that, which is lonely,
Thinking how strangely things come about.
When your letter—your womanly letter
Was placed in my hand—need I say
That its face (for I knew 'twas from you, dear),
Smiled away the fatigue of the day.

You may guess how I read and reread it
And dwelt on each word; well I knew
Ere 'twas opened no words but those truest
Would be found in a letter from you—
And reading you seemed to be with me
Once more and your heart's truth divine,
Which e'er beamed in your eyes when beside you,
Shone forth in your words line by line.

To be sure 'twas amusing to see you
Write so freely of such brilliant scenes—
Of Beaux—and in sooth a proposal
From a youngster just out of his teens—
All of which pleased me more than you fancy,
—The dances, soirées, and all that—
That is, since " the belle of the season "
From it all turned to "Poverty flat."

Then the drive in the park, in a turnout
Like that of a princess in state—
Yet you still think our drive was "the rarest "
From old Harrison's barn to the gate?
Well, you're not very wrong—and I'm thinking
That in "rarest " you have the right word
For the reason—if rightly I guess it,
That our hearts were in rarest accord.

Yes, our happiness here was complete, Su',
Or seemed so, and that's all the same,
Till the metal was struck in the placer,
And the gold fairly rolled from the claim;
Then of course there was nothing to keep you
Out here in the mud at the " Fork,"
So the grocery was sold and the "diggin's "
Were exchanged for the scenes of New-York.

Two years since have passed—all continues
Pretty much as when last you were here—
Some have "struck it," but most are still striving
With little to eat or to wear,
Much less finding gold, or, perhaps, only
Enough to give prospect of more—
But most have but little to hope for,
And just strive to keep want from the door.

And who, do you ask, are the finders;
And how rich are the new paying *leads?*
Well some who began in the ditches
And some who began at the *feeds;*
And some of our five—you remember
From Hampshire, at last are repaid;
You recall how three years past they came here
Recruits for "the digger brigade!"

There's old Dobson: you know his last penny
Was gone when you left—well, they say
His share in the Davenport placer
Is worth twenty thousand to-day—
"Clean money?" O, no—twenty thousand
Every month it holds out—you may guess
How the girls have dropped cotton and gingham
And taken to silks for their dress.

And then, I had almost forgotten (?)
Another rich *strike* has been made
Where the gold merely has to be lifted
Without labor of pick or of spade:
Two months past 'twas struck up the mountains—
Two years since the "digger" began;
The result? Some few thousands to credit,—
Can't you guess who's the fortunate man?

Do you know him?—well, let me remember—
Why, certain you do—don't you know
"That unlucky digger" named Danvers—
Joseph Danvers—more commonly Joe?
That's me, Su',—what, don't you believe it?
No wonder—I didn't myself
Till I knew the North Bank to my credit
Held a round fifty thousand of pelf.

Yes, fifty and further take notice
That I've sold out the claim as it stands
For five hundred thousand gold, minted,
And the checks have passed under my hands—
Ah, my Beauty, how little you fancied
In the midst of your fashion and glare
That the man whom you loved as a "digger"
Was that unlucky Joe—millionaire!

HIS REPLY.

What next?

        —In two weeks I reach Denver,
And forever good-bye to " the Fork:"
And thence fast as wheels can whirl eastward
I'll be with you, dear, in New York,
And then we'll be finished by travel
And learn what it means, and all that,
And our joy shall be none the less telling
For the memories of " Poverty flat."

So good night and good-bye for a little,
Altho' you're asleep as I write,
For ten on this slope, if I err not,
In your quarter is three in the night—
Yet once more good night and be happy
Henceforth and forever and know
There is one who will strive so to make you,
Joseph Danvers—more commonly

                  JOE.

THE EARLY WORM,

OF UNHAPPY MEMORY.

I.

Oft hath been told the ancient tale
  Yclept "the early bird,"
But with great naughtiness the truth
  Hath been but half averred.

II.

Once on a time a little worm,—
  Thus should the story run,—
Arose with unsuspecting trust
  To greet the rising sun.

III.

Forth from his snug retreat he set
  Hard by a moss-grown wood;
And whistled gaily as he went—
  Or *would have* if he could.

IV.

He gained the mead and soon upon
  A hollow log he *gat*,   ·
Which well he knew for oft thereon
  In the warm sun he sat

V.

And slept, curled in a little ball,
  For be it known that he
Was not a common worm, but of
  The old Grub famil*ee*.

VI.

Full pleased was he with his own self
  And as the sun arose,
He felt like juveniles who feel
  Too big for their small clo"es.

VII.

But soon into his ear there crèpt
  A bird's sweet minstrelsy,
Which pleased him so that he fell to
  And danced right merrily.

VIII.

Alack the day! The warbler spied
  The all too giddy mite,
And while he loved to trill full well
  A worm was his delight!

IX.

He dropped his song, the better on
  His helpless prey to drop;
Then, though his victim strove to fly,
  He popped him in his crop!

X.

Thus it befell; that hapless worm,
  So good, so prompt at morn
Was by his very virtues thus
  From life and pleasure torn.

XI.

Yet but himself to blame, for if
  He had but kept his bed
To rise betimes, some other worm
  Would have been swallow-*ed!*

NIGHT.

Thou orb sublime that from the boundless sky
  Night's darkening curtain now dost upward roll !
And flood'st the world in balmful brilliancy
  That steals like dream-hushed music on the soul,

From this still height, amid the breathless grove,
  Whereon thou dost thy first soft brightness shed,
I watch thee rise with an adoring love,
  Thou queen of light in majesty arrayed!

Above yon looming cliff, whose sombre height,
  Black 'gainst the sky, o'erlooks the slumbering sea,
Thou soar'st aloft, dissolving into light
  The waters, cradled to tranquility.

Mounting on high soon doth thy radiance fill
  The earth and sea—most welcome on the deep
Where thy bright beams with hope all wanderers
      thrill
  Who in the night across the ocean sweep.

Yonder the distant city sleeps, revealed by thee,
  As thou dost silver dome and spire there:
Whence now, scarce heard above the murmuring sea,
  The midnight bell steals o'er the slumbering air.

As thy full beams disperse night's gathered gloom
  'Mid its dark scenes, what haunts of misery there;
What drear abodes of anguish they illume,
  Sunk in the rayless midnight of despair!

What thoughts disturb the lonely convict's heart
  As now he views thee from his ironed cell,
Of childhood's days; of cherished hopes depart,
  Which he remembers—ah, too sadly well.

He feels thy beams, as now *his* night they invade,
  Rest on a scene which memory weeps to trace:
A grave amid the village church-yard's shade,
  Of her who sank beneath a child's disgrace.

Thus, what diversity of scene untold
  Dost thou behold; what mighty empires sway
Hast seen, as through long ages thou hast rolled,
  As now thou roll'st unchanged—yet where are
      they?

Where now is haughty Babylonia's might
Which madly dared Omnipotence deride?
For thou hast too illumed her guilty site
As now the plain which sepulchres her pride!

So shall thy beams, before another sun,
Look on the walls of crumbling Pompeii,
And from the heights of silent Lebanon
Flood the still waves of holy Galilee.

*　　*　　*　　*

Infinite theme! Thou God all-powerful,
Whose hand directs e'en as Thy hand hath made
The Universe stupendous! who may tell
The countless wonders of Thy work displayed.

UNKNOWN SOLDIER.

Ye patriot dead! o'er your sleep of devotion
  Beams the proud star of victory, all gloriously
      bright!
Here by the dark stream, winding down to the ocean
  Which beheld you go forth in the pride of your
      might.

Full its radiance illumines the shades which enfold
      you,
  Reflecting your glory—which brightens its ray,—
In the hearts which forever with pride shall behold
      you,
Through ages to come as through years passed
      away.

And can it then be that "unknown" ye are sleeping
  By the fields of your valor, so fearlessly trod?
Can a Nation forget that the fruits she is reaping
  Are sprung from the soil warmed to life by thy
      blood?

Ye *are* known : by the hearts which—sorrow e'er at-
    tending—
Your memory embalm in love's holiest perfumes ;
By the tears of a Nation which o'er you descending
    Refresh the sweet flowers that wave o'er your
    tombs.

Thus not here, where the bleak winds in rude lamen-
    tation
    Complainingly wander among the sad pine,
Are you tombed, but your graves the warm hearts of
    a Nation,
    Where evergreen blooming, love's memories twine.

No more shall the thunders of battle elate you ;
    No more shall the trumpet of victory thrill—
Till the last trumpet's sound, which forever shall
    wake you,
    When *known* ye shall rise to the life immortal.

ON THE SANDS.

A proud ship northward sailing,
Across a shadowed sea,—
As lonely as love forbidden
The haven where it would be.

On the sands two forms are lingering ;
'Gainst the rock of their destiny,
The tides of their hearts are swelling
Like the waves of a troubled sea.

For a gulf has been fixed between them,
By the changeless decree of Fate :
After long years of waiting,
Found—but, alas, too late.

Yet ne'er shall those tides of feeling
Rest till each heart be at peace,
As not till Time's consummation,
Shall the tides of ocean cease.

For they roll from Truth's vast ocean
That infinite, changeless sea,
And the power that directs their pulses
    Is immutable Deity.

Oh life! O fate! O sorrow!
Must love's true currents flow
Side by side, like companion rivers
That never a mingling know?

Then a voice, blent with ocean's, answers:—
Not here 'neath earth's changeful skies
Can love be made perfect,—but yonder
    In the field's of paradise.

TO A CANARY.

Who fashioned thy exquisite symmetry,
  Thou little fay of song, thou paragon
Of grace; what wondrous cunning artisan
  The texture wove of thy bright livery?

What hand the delicate machinery cast
  Whereby thou mov'st with such unerring skill?
Who in thy tiny frame the forces placed,
  Which make it all-obedient to thy will?

What hast thou in that little throat of thine
  To trill such notes of dulcet purity?
Who taught thee thus in minstrelsy divine
  To pour thy soul in rhythmic ecstacy?

Perchance it was in thine own native shades,
  The purling brook, the voices of the woods,
Where now thy fellows in bright flow'ry glades,
  Fill with sweet song their island solitudes.

But these *thou* ne'er hast known; then 't was thy sire
　Tuned thy sweet voice?   Nay, loud thy warblings
　　tell,
In praises rising softly, sweetly higher,
　'Twas nature's God that fashioned thee so well!

Would I could tell thee how I love thy song;
　How dear to me, thou lovely one, thou art.
Why fly'st thou from me?   I but fondly long
　With kindliest hand to lay thee to my heart.

How happily would'st thou lie upon this breast,
　Did'st thou but know how warms my heart to thee;
Now, captive there, in thy sweet eyes' unrest,
　Pained I behold thou fain would'st fly from me.

Thou can'st not understand my words, I know,
　But love hath many voices, and for thee
Nature hath surely purposed one, and so
　I am content, for Time will teach it me.

MONA.

How can I paint thy beauties; how relate
  Thy virtues? words to compass them so fail
Thy graces—e'en the cadence of thy feet,
  Make affluent Speech a poverty reveal,
Language too poor to justly celebrate
  The temple of thy form ; the grace to tell
Of its fair priestess, matchless ! Sight alone
  Can know how perfect Beauty's paragon!

It may not be that peerless music's strain
  More richly sounds since I have known thy love ;
It may not be fair Dian with her train
  Of stars refulgent, in her course above
Now brighter beams; yet music's loved refrain
  Far sweeter is ; yon orbs—*all* things now prove
Sources of joy undreamt, and to life yield
  Rich springs of beauty ne'er before revealed.

E'en as the sun with its resplendent light
 Doth flood the world in nameless radiancy;
Raising all sunk in darkness by the night
 To share the glory of his majesty,
So shall thy love impart a new delight
 To every joy, and life's ambitions be
Exalted to a nobler aim, and yet—
 Nay, thy sweet eyes rebuke that thought—*forget!*

'Mid their soft depths, dark as the star-filled skies,
 As 'mid the night heat's silent lightnings play
In quivering warmth, love's flames reflected rise
 From the altar thy heart hath built to me.
And there shall love with gladness sacrifice
 This self it hath bound captive, for to thee   .
Who has enthroned love's image in my breast,
 'Twould consecrate the life thou thus hast blest !

As 't were from sleep thou'st waked me ; changed to
  day
 The darkness of the past,—appearing now
How dark ! And thence emerged all wondrously
 This new-found world breaks glorious on the view,
And circling all—as doth the earth the sky!
 Love doth encompass this creation new,
Of which thou art the Queen, a soverignty
 In which thou'st crowned me Consort unto thee !

A THOUGHT.

I watched a rose at evening fade away,
  As leaf by leaf its crimson richness fell,
And sadly gazing thought, may thus decay
  Such beauty claim, thence irredeemable?

I sought in vain the multitudinous dew,
  An hour before glitt'ring in bright array
Along the sward, nor aught was left to show
  What glory thence had passed from earth away!

The spirit of the flower, the soul, methought,
  Of fire in the dew, thus fled, must pass
To some bright realm, and straight my fancy sought
  To place the sphere worthy such loveliness.

To *Phosphor* floating in her sea of light—
  An isle of glory; to th' enchanted sphere
Arched by the iris; to each star its flight
  Did Fancy wing—successless voyager.

        *   *   *   *

I stood amid a scene of brilliant joy,
   Where Beauty moved, in Music's sweet embrace,
Shedding on all a nameless radiancy
   From the divine effulgence of her face!

Then Love exultant cried: "That fit repose
   By Fancy sought, e'en here all glorious view:
In Beauty's cheek immortal blooms the rose;
   In Beauty's eyes the fires born in the dew!"

MUSIC AND MEMORY.

Music once wandering through the heart,
  As daylight died away,
Found Memory sleeping by a tomb
  Whose verdure withering lay.

Whispering she touched the slumberer,
  Soft as the moon's pale beam
The folded flower, then passed away
  As vanishes a dream.

Memory awoke and caught the voice
  Re-echoing plaintively,
Then, weeping, viewed where she had slept,
  And oh, how bitterly!

And now, no greener spot is there
  For Memory loves to twine
The richest verdure of the heart
  Around that sacred shrine.

A REMEMBRANCE.

I stood alone on the pebbled beach
  As the moon rose over the sea,
And the doleful break of the restless waves,
  Brought sad memories to me.

Across her silvery path o'er the wave
  A ship passed into the night;
Though it glided by ere I'd viewed it well,
  I can never forget that sight.

E'en thus, I thought, on life's path appear
  Sweet faces a moment seen,
Then lost to us: a grave in the heart
  Which memory keeps ever green.

THE DAKOTA.

A FRAGMENT.

I.

Far 'neath the crimson west, all sear and brown,
  Range the dark hills of the Dakota land,
By arid plains; yet farther, looking down
  On pine-gloomed wilds, where waters darkly grand
Leap their rock-walls.   There wide the wind-drift
      sand,
  The ashen alkali, stretches a-plain,
O'er which, else shadeless, sun-scorched sparsely
      stand
  The lonely cotton-woods; and as a-main
Ships' sailless masts, becalmed, 'neath burning skies,
From 'far appear, their slender heights arise.

II.

There in primitive lodges of the plain,
  Dwelt the Dakota tribes confederate,
The land possessing 'twixt the rock-forged chain
  Of mountains westward and the river great,
"Father of waters" named, which through the gate

Of Delta rolls into the southern sea.
Foremost in war, with courage desperate,
  Of all the mightiest braves most dreaded they,
Till in defence 'gainst them combined arose
Tribes which else held themselves deadliest of foes!

III.

For countless years, free as the wingèd wind,
  And scarce less fleet; more fierce and deadlier far,
O'er plain and through deep forests, rock-confined
  To dauntless strength most loved, the Savage there
Ranged chieftain of the wilds.   Alike the lair
  Of mountain beast and eagles' eyried bed,
Far up the crag, 't was but his joy to dare;
  And oft the grizzly monster crouched in dread
Of such a foe, till desperate driven at length
Employed, how vainly, its else matchless strength!

IV.

Swift, not less sure, the barbèd arrow flew
  From his sprung bow, drawn 'neath a strength like
    that
Which in the storm the stoutest sapling, low
  Bends earthward; in the fated life to wet
Its lightning shaft, with feathery rudders set,
  Plucked from the wing which soaring high it
    brought

Lifeless to lay low at its master's feet—
  His gladdest triumph save when true it sought
The hostile's breast, to yield him that e'er still
The proudest trophy of a warrior's skill!

V.

In verdured plains, walled by the mountain height,
  Beside the running waters was his home,
Where rose, scarce fewer than a countless flight
  Of winged-ones north-bound when the spring has
    come,
The painted tepees of his tribe.   Close some
  Stood 'neath the mount; some by the river's sands,
Where, tethered, danced in the in-eddying foam
  The swift canoes,—some staunch for war's de-
    mands;
Some of a grace, with odorous cedar wings,
But fitted for love's happy wanderings.

VI.

And oft it was when the last beams of day
  Bathed stream and woodland in their soft rose-
    hue,
As the bright moon, with love-inspiring ray,
  Floated, all beauteous, up the orient blue,
Out from the shore glided the light canoe

Bearing the love-led warrior, proudly plumed,
And Indian maid, clad in the softest doe,
　Feathered and fringed, her olive breast illumed
With rustic gems, his gift, by daring brought
From nature's stores, o'er ways with dangers fraught.

VII.

Now when the vernal tide its riches spread
　O'er the north pampas, and the bison came,
In bands forth issuing, fleetly mounted, sped
　The younger braves to take the pasturing game.
Armed with the bow and spear, each eye a-gleam.
　Looking impatient courage, crested high
With eagle plumes stained to a crimson flame,
　Shouting exultant, 'gainst the evening sky
O'er the west hills they dashed and far away,
To strike the feeding herds ere dawn of day.

VIII.

On their fleet coursers of the wild astride
　At morn—kept by the single, scarce touched rein,
Now half unhorsed—o'er-leaning low aside,
　Quick straight a-mount, alike they swept the plain,
As now they charged the flying herd, which ta'en
　Surprised, by cunning artifice, swift fled
A surging mass,—the blackened, trembling plain

And rolling prairie thundering 'neath their tread,
Till it did seem like some dark inland sea
Wrought from beneath to tumult suddenly!

IX.

Children of Nature, bounteous she supplied
  Their wants, nor wished they aught she gave them
      not,—
The stretching plains their country, and the wide
  Skies circling the sole bound their science taught,
Swift retribution e'er the guilty sought,
  And justice dealt—their law the law of heaven,
Through ages past to them tradition brought,
  By the Great Spirit to their fathers given;
Confirmed to them whene'er in thunders loud
His voice they heard from 'midst the flame-rent
    cloud!

*   *   *   *

UNDERLEY.

Fair hills and dales in summer's wealth arrayed,
On every side adorned with richest shade;
Along the vale, o'er pebbles white and gray,
The river babbling on its winding way
By cliff and woodland, and 'neath arches seared,
Which Roman skill to outlive centuries reared,
And to the distant sea still circling on,
Crooning its story of long ages gone.

Upsloping from the marge to park and grange,
Rare pastures where the lowing beauties range
With fleece-white herds which o'er the greenswards
     rove,
Or clustering, drowse within the leafy grove.

A garden set in graceful, terraced frames,
Whose every line the hand of Art proclaims,
Where countless flowers blossom everywhere,
And breathe their fragrance on the slumbrous air.

Alone, and grouped, old trees of stately mien,
And, fringed with colour, copses softly green—
The haunts of birds, which with the quiet breeze
Blend their soft notes in dulcet harmonies.

Embowered in the midst, a stately home:
    Grey tower and turret rising o'er the land,
Lined by the circling years as they have come
    And passed away—albeit with gentlest hand.

Ideal scenes where Nature, Art delight
To soothe the soul—to charm the lingering sight:
In memory's shrine, where all most loved is laid,
Fixing a picture which can never fade.

Such is the prospect I have found in thee;
Such is thy beauty, noble Underley.

Westmoreland, 1890.

LOVE IN ABSENCE.

"En el amor la auscencia es como el aire, que apaga el
fuego chico, e enciende el grande."
—Spanish Proverb.

A little fire
Must soon expire
'Neath the wind's agitation,
Whereas the same
A greater flame
Swells to a conflagration!

E'en so to love
Doth absence prove:
A little fire o'er-turning,
But when the breast
Love's flames invest,
It sets them wildly burning.

THE DYING FLOWER.

—

Tu ne vis qu' un jour,
Disait le buisson à la rose.

—LeBailly.

" Sweet flower, and must thy beauty fade,
   Though born but yesterday ?
Scarce one short day of life, and now
   Thou hasten'st to decay."

" True, brief is my abiding here,"
   Replied the flower, "and yet
If earth be sweeter for my life
   I know naught of regret."

———

THE EGOTIST.

Epitaph from the French.

—

Here lies a man who ne'er did good or bad;
Loved but himself—and not a rival had.

A TOAST.

In the grape's golden glow an oblation
To Beauty—supreme paragon!
Wanting whom life would be as in darkness
Notwithstanding the light of the sun;
Lovely woman! the queen of the ages,
A sovereign whose heralds proclaim
That all kings, princes, prelates and sages
Are rulers of earth but in name!

Her eyes ?—who shall fathom the secret
Of the power enthroned there alway!
Her voice ?—in all harmonies riches
Naught so wondrous to move or allay;
Her form ?—the one shrine where all worship
Since the sweep of the centuries began;
So a health—a libation befitting
The darling—the idol of man!

She alone the one source of all joyance;
To her presence all sorrow defers;
Earth's shadows she silvers with brightness;
In the sunlight the brilliance is hers!
So once more and forever we pledge her
From the fountain that sparkles with light,
The gift of the Gods for the goddess
Who shall reign while the years keep their flight !

LINES IN AN ALBUM.

Spotless this page where now my verse I place;
E'en thus the record of thy young life is.
Would that as here friendship I fondly trace
I *there* might grave enduring happiness.

THE SAME.

In her high temple Memory shall enshrine,—
As love hath in the temple of the heart,—
Thy image 'neath that of the Muse divine,
Whose votary and favored child thou art.

THE SAME.

As when beneath the church-yard's quiet shade
We wander musing at the close of day,
And mark the sadd'ning records telling there
Of fondest friendships which have passed away;
So in life's evening when thine eyes shall stray
Amid these pages, to thy memory dear,
Pass not *this* leaf—in friendship's sacred name
Fondly I now inscribe "remembrance" here.

The Same

Goodness is thy beauty's dower
Unobtrusive as the flower
   Shadowed in the lea;
Silvery as the brooklet's trebles
Flowing o'er enamelled pebbles
   Sounds thy voice to me.

The Same.

My autograph you ask?   Behold
Upon this page I gladly write it.
May smiles alone attend the lips
At whose command I now indite it.

LINES

Written in the fly leaf of a book presented to Dr. —— on his
return to his home in Bermuda.

With this adieu—alas that jealous Fate
Should ever thus fond friendships separate!
Mayst thou and thine by joy e'er compassed be
As are thine isles by their glad, sunlit sea.

SONGS.

JACK AT THE OAR.

All merrily
O'er the billows free
Our light boat swiftly glides,
And the mellow light
Of the starry night
Our course o'er the water guides.
With thoughts as free
As the rolling sea,
O'er the tossing waves we bound,
While in the deep,
As we onward sweep,
Our oars fall with musical sound!

CHORUS.

Then row with a will, with a will, boys,
And sing as we go with a will, boys!
Our strength to the oar, speeding on to the shore
O'er the sea we love as we e'er will, boys.

The winds we brave,
While the bounding wave
Obedient to our will,

Like a mettled steed
From its curbings freed,
Bears us onward—onward still !
The waves may dash,
The lightnings flash,
And the winds oppose our course—
These our joy to dare,
Their wild sport to share,
As we mingle our voices with theirs !

CHORUS.

Now the moon above
Waking thoughts of love,
Fills the scene with her dreamy light,
As within the bay,—
Passed the open sea,—
We glide o'er the wavelets bright.
And a steady oar
Speeds us to the shore,
While our hearts' warmest pulses move,
For we know that there
Wait us faces dear,
Whose smiles are the guerdon of love.

CHORUS.

SONG.

A sky of purest sapphire,
A shore of silver sand;
The constant ocean whispering
Its love unto the land.
A sail all solitary
Drifting across the sea,
As hearts drift on in silence,
Unknown their destiny.

REFRAIN.

Beauteous, ah beauteous, earth and sea and air,
Yet joy my spirit finds not anywhere;
Patience, O, faithful heart, e'en as day follows night
And darkness is resolved to beams of radiant light,
 So shall the shadows pass
 And joy replace the sorrow,
 Patiently—hopefully,
 So shall gladness come to thee.

II.

In vision-land we linger,
Hope's dream is pictured there;
We call: no voice in answer;
We wake and all is drear—
When shall the shadows vanish
And life be at its best;
When shall the heart's fond longings
In joy's completeness rest?

REFRAIN.

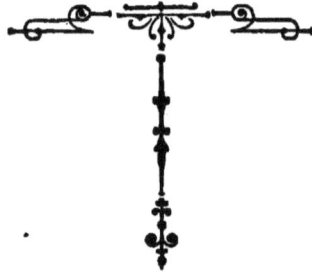

I Love to Look Into Thine Eyes.

I love to look into thine eyes,
　Thy soul's bright mirrors, where
Its crystal depths reflected beam—
　Glancing in beauty there !

I love to look into thine eyes,
　Sweet springs which, sparkling o'er
Life's arid plain, refreshment yield
　Else never known before.

I love to look into thine eyes
　Where virtues mirrored are;
Virtues which Modesty would hide
　By Truth revealèd there.

SONG.

—

Love hath my heart a garden made,
   Therein where all was bare,
Beneath his magic husbandry
   Rich blooms of beauty rare
Profusely spring, and such a wealth
   Of incense yields each flower,
A sweet intoxication fills
   With rapture every hour.

So at his bidding day by day
   Shall gentle Constancy,
The rarest blooms untiring cull
   And bring them unto thee;
And at thy feet shall lay them sweet,—
   Whence Love bids thee to bear
Them to thy heart, that they may find
   A life immortal there.

SONG.

There's some one with the brightest eyes
That ever love betrayed;
There's some one with the sweetest smile
That beauty e'er displayed,
Whose image, wheresoe'er I be,
Love ever brings to view,
And who that some one is, fairest,
I scarce need *name* to you.

There is an anxious heart that knows
A rapture it conceals,
And longing waits the hour to speak
The fullness which it feels.
Its joy alone beneath that smile,
'Neath those sweet eyes of blue,
And in whose breast it beats, sweet one,
Oh, need I name to you?

MUSIC AND ITS PROCESSES.

MUSIC AND ITS PROCESSES.

Notwithstanding the marvelous perfection to which music has beeen brought in all its branches, and the very exhaustive treatises which have been written on the theories of the art, not to speak of the wonderful mastery which has been obtained over its technical difficulties, psychologically considered, the subject does not appear to have received an equal degree of attention other than in works too voluminous, if not too abstruse, for general reading. Our purpose in this paper will be to inquire briefly into the processes of the several FACTORS in music as relates to their effect upon the listener; and if we can succeed in throwing some light on the subject for "the great majority," we shall not have labored in vain, even though we fail to "extend the horizon" of the more knowing few.

In undertaking to offer an answer to the question, "How does music act upon its auditor to impart that pleasure which it so universally affords?" it is

(143)

important to have in mind two facts. First, that this pleasure, in its aggregate, is a complex emotion, comprising many simple emotions, which latter, it may be suggested, consist of still other more subtle refinements of feeling. Thus our inquiry must be into the nature of those primary factors in music and their processes which give rise to the individual emotions ; and if we can trace out these, we shall have gone far toward reaching an understanding of the subject presented. The second fact is that the high distinguishing power of creative minds, in the arts in general, is that faculty which enables them to go beyond personal experiences and to comprehend the whole range of human emotions (of which we have the highest example in the art of Shakespeare), which faculty, as need scarcely be suggested, is the god-like attribute of genius.

As all understand, among the arts, music takes a high place as an exponent of the emotions, which indeed was its primitive, as it has ever been its chief mission ; its first crude forms having been no more than the spontaneous utterance of human feeling.

And just here let us direct attention to the identity and consequent immediate relation which exists between the inherent properties of music and those of emotion, which need only to be mentioned to be at once recognized,—pointed out by Dr. Haweis, in his able book, " Music and Morals."

These properties, both in music and emotion, have been identified as velocity, intensity, complexity, elation and depression, which in the respective cases may be approximated as follows :

IN MUSIC.

VELOCITY by the several *tempi* employed, as various as are numerous the degrees in the range included within the terms *largo* and *prestissimo*.

INTENSITY by the infinitely minute gradations possible between the signs *ppp* and *fff*.

COMPLEXITY by the countless subtly interwoven quantities of harmony worked upon the web of melody.

ELATION AND DEPRESSION by the tones and their intervals as treated and developed by the composer and interpreted by the performer.

IN EMOTION.

VELOCITY by successive impulses of feeling such as are experienced in situations which excite a series of emotions, following each other in various degrees of velocity.

INTENSITY by the various degrees in which feeling sways us, ranging from the simplest emotion, which may be all but neutral, to the condition of highest excitability.

COMPLEXITY by a concatenation of emotions, which succeed each other at a rate of velocity so great that even the "lightning of the mind" may scarcely distinguish where one state of feeling ceases and the next begins ; the appreciable result of which is the complete, complex sensation, or "complexity."

ELATION AND DEPRESSION by the various states of feeling, ranging from the lowest despondency to the top-most heights of exultation.

Thus are suggested corresponding planes between music and emotion, and these will assist us in tracing out the processes by which one acts upon the other.

As the primary, and consequently fundamental constituent of music, we consider melody first in order, and, secondly, its grand accessory and beautifier, harmony; for it is melody which serves in the art as the articulate voice-medium of expression, as relates to emotion, becoming, under the inspiration of the composer, the embodiment, so to speak, of particular states of mind and feeling. By *melody* is of course understood the rhythmic progression of notes, as distinguished from the grouping of notes or harmony.

It may be safely premised that most of us who have reached the years of maturity have experienced all of what may be termed the fundamental human emotions, varying, of course, in intensity and continuity, with the susceptibility of the nature acted upon, and modified by attendant circumstances. Of these emotions, rising from time to time, those with which it is the peculiar province of music to deal do not always find commensurate expression, and this is particularly true of those tender sentiments with which music so continually employs itself, which emotions are afforded but partial expression, or lie voiceless within, ever ready to welcome opportunity for expression. As it is true that the major portion of mankind have at least touched upon the fundamental emotions common to humanity, so, conversely, is it true that all human emotion has been given expression to through the respective media of art by the master-workers therewith; and this may be said of music alone within the limitations of the art. Thus it follows that all who can place themselves in sympathy with music (and who cannot?) may find therein expression for the higher emotions of the soul, inarticulate though it be as compared with the art of speech, while at the same time it is doubtless true that music serves as a medium of expression for deep-lying refinements of feeling, too subtle for the symbols of speech.

It is not unusual to meet in the course of our reading, with a thought which we at once recognize as one which we have ourselves before known—in many instances, perhaps, in an equally positive form as that in which we find it preserved. It may be, however, that we have not given it expression, or if at all, we have not uttered it with any special definiteness. Some of the thoughts, however, which may thus be recognized have presented themselves so evanescently to our consciousness that we can hardly claim them as our own ; their outline only having passed before our mental vision without leaving any distinct impression, just as the prepared plate in the camera may be said to receive an imperfect outline only of an object if submitted to it but for an instant. Yet, again, we can conceive that there are still other thoughts in embryo which have only just reached the border line of consciousness, as yet on the nether side, but the moment these come in contact with their related expression they become quickened into action, as the electric spark springs forth the moment the complete conductor touches its source ; up to that instant remaining motionless though living. In like manner we conceive it to be the case with feeling. From the most neutral to those most actively alive, are there emotions waiting upon expression ; their permanent, unfathomable nature, making repeated expression ever welcome to them,—which, indeed, may be said, with more or less truth, of all emotion. Others have been but partially expressed, while again there are those (if we may be allowed to anticipate their existence) which like the thought in embryo, have not as yet taken their definite form, but which, when brought in con-

tact with their adequate conductor, become vivified
and produce their corresponding sensation.

May it not be that those nameless emotions which
are experienced when we come under the influence of
certain passages in the music of such magicians in
the art as Beethoven, which we are unable satisfac-
torily to fix or define to our understanding, belong
to the class last named, which, undefined though
they be, afford us a pleasure of a very positive, albeit mysterious character. If the doctrine of metem-
psychosis were admissible, these stranger emotions
might be accounted for by supposing them to per-
tain to some prior condition of existence ; emotions
which such music as that named, alone, is capable
of awakening or giving utterance to in this present
existence.

Admitting the theory that the master-workers in
the art under consideration have comprehended all
human feeling, and created therefor adequate channels of expression, it follows that when we place our
selves under the influence of the art, in the hands of
the interpreter, the latent or active feeling responds
thereto, affording that pleasurable sensation which
the expression of emotion always yields.

Let us apply our premises. In listening to a musical composition, we recognize it as dealing with some
given sentiment. Not, perhaps, apprehending the
exact phase of the sentiment treated, but the fundamental emotion to which it is related, and therefore

one which, accepting the hypothesis submitted, each auditor has already experienced in some degree,—hence recognizes. Thus identified, our emotional nature responds thereto in various degrees in each individual as such of their several experiences as harmonize with the given sentiment vary—for as the composer colors the emotion interpreted with his own individuality, so does each auditor receive such interpretation in its application to his own particular experience ; and more or less intense as the emotional nature prevails in the case of each listener respectivly.

Furthermore, the effect will, of course, be in proportion as the composer possesses a nature capable of feeling and power to adequately interpret through his art the given emotion.

Each auditor thus recognizing (by the intuition of feeling rather than by any intellectual apprehension) in the given theme the expression of a more or less familiar emotion, which, in the particular case, may never have found adequate, or but partial utterance, the emotional being which, so to speak, has been bearing the burden of the unuttered feeling, gladly welcomes and rests itself upon that expression, making it its own, and thus is experienced that sense of satisfaction the ultimate of which we know as pleasure.

Not only is it true, as has been said, that all mankind have experienced, in various degrees, the fun-

damental feelings of our human nature, but it is
also the fact that all have known something of the
more exalted emotions,—such, for example, as those
of the sublime, the heroic, and the like; and it is
more particularly true of these that in this mater-
ialistic age they but seldom find exercise except
that which may be termed the sympathetic expression afforded when we come under the influence
of art.

Thus, such music as represents martial cadences,
the pageantry of arms, or as relates to the more re-
ligio-sublime, those grand choral-form progressions
and magnificent passages, as in Oratorio, which we in-
tuitively recognize as the utterance of emotion per-
taining to the most exalted planes of feeling,—(to
which the highest natures alone may attain), may be
said to awaken that profound sentiment which
springs worshipfully from the apprehension of the
divine conceptions presented in these grander crea-
tions of the art, and afford an expression to the sub-
limer emotions which elsewise for the most part
they know not ; and the man or woman with but little of the religious or heroic in their nature, may by
this agency be moved to a depth which no other influence might ever reach.   Under the influence of
this class of music, which excites the heroic sentiment, we feel that pleasure which a quickening of the
nobler impulses of the soul affords, while in the latter case, where the religious sentiment is brought

into action, the soul is subdued into a state of devotion and repose, or exalted by the sentiment of rev-
erence and adoration.

Moreover, it is to be remembered, that this pleasure is largely aided by the " association process,"
which contributes in an important degree to the
pleasure experienced (as it does indeed in most processes of mind), industriously gathering about such
pleasurable feeling, as a given theme or passage may
awaken, all experiences in consonance therewith,
which add their coloring to the dominant emotion.

Herein, then, seems to lie the primary source of
the pleasure afforded by music: that it is an articulate voice, whereby we may find more or less adequate expression for the deepest emotions which
inhabit the unfathomable recesses of the soul. Over
and beyond the delectation which is thus derived
from what may be termed the soul of music, there
is a supplementary pleasure afforded by the external
forms of melody. This clearly arises from the perception, in its numerous rhythmic designs and
varying cadences, of the beauty of symmetry, proportion and the like thereby outlined before the
mind, while at the same time, by the process of as-
similation, may be suggested some of the multitudinous rhythms in the world of nature, or some
other of its more sublime manifestations. And here
again is the " association process " found occupying
itself, calling up before the mind the scenes where

such manifestations are known, thus giving rise to other simple emotions, each contributing its pleasurable sensation; the aggregate of all being the "complex" or complete pleasure.

Moreover, the external forms of melody delight us by their supplementary elaboration and embellishment, affording a pleasure very similar to, if indeed not identical with that experienced in contemplating the graceful or fantastic designs of line and curve wrought into delicate arabesques and infinite forms of beauty in a sister art.

Let us accept melody, then, as the prime source of that pleasure which music affords; not, of course, wishing to be understood that melody *per se* affords this pleasure, but that, as presented in musical compositions, it is the *primary* factor which produces the pleasurable emotion experienced. First, as being the embodied expression of human feeling, that is the *soul* of it; and, secondly, by its external beauty of form and embellishment, all interwoven by harmony into the perfect whole.

A brief word may be added as to harmony, which is understood to be the combination of two or more notes bearing relative consistent proportions to the fundamental tone. The meed of pleasure which harmony contributes to the aggregate derived from music, plainly results from the character and *color* which it imparts to, and incidentally from the rich vestments, so to speak, woven from its " concord of sweet sounds," in which it robes its subject.

As presented to the imagination, its innumerable combinations of beauty delight us now by their embroider-like richness; following which the imagination is conducted amid ingeniously developed progressions, from one enchanting surprise to another; now dazzling by their regal splendor, scintillating with rich decoration as might the brilliant caparisons of a royal pageant glistening in the sunlight— awakening the more pleasurable phases of wonder and admiration, or again by their closely interwoven, yet, in point of continuance, broadly extended beauty, through which run the golden threads of melody, suggesting to the mind the velvety richness of superb tapestries, into which are woven uniquely delicate or boldly figured designs, and unnumbered other mental pictures of beauty, giving rise to other various and amplified phases of the emotions named, and so forth. All these harmonic variations, infinite in number, being consistently proportioned and combined, now in powerful contrasts, or again in the most delicate interfusions of sound, their effect upon the sensibilities may be said to be related to that experienced in contemplating perfect combinations, gradations and interblending of colors, especially if in action as in a fine sunset, as when viewed across an expanse of water, upon which the rich masses of color are cradled into innumerable combinations of beauty. In this connection is recalled the thought suggested by the author already quoted, that the time may come when ingenuity will have devised instruments whereby *color* may be manipulated and expressed in rhythmic action and harmonic combinations, *i. e.*, symphonies in color, which shall impart the same pleasure through the sense of sight that we now derive from symphonies in sound.

We have sought thus briefly to outline the view that the pleasure derived from music is chiefly produced by its fundamental constituent, melody:

1st. As furnishing an adequate medium of expression to the most noble, most tender and consequently most demandful of human emotions; the importance of which service makes apparent the divineness of its mission.

2nd. By the countless designs of beauty presented to the mind in its various and ever varying forms.

3rd. By the rich ornamentation and embellishments it displays.

4th. By calling into action the "association process" which calls up before the mind that which diverts and delights, and

Finally, that harmony, the grand auxiliary and beautifier of melody, contributes in a preëminent degree to heighten, and to create, the sum total of pleasure afforded, in the manner briefly indicated.